The Run of the Tide

Patrick Stephens Limited, part of Thorsons, a division of the Collins Publishing Group, has published authoritative, quality books for enthusiasts for more than twenty years. During that time the company has established a reputation as one of the world's leading publishers of books on aviation, maritime, military, model-making, motor cycling, motoring, motor racing, railway and railway modelling subjects. Readers or authors with suggestions for books they would like to see published are invited to write to: The Editorial Director, Patrick Stephens Limited, Thorsons Publishing Group, Wellingborough, Northants, NN8 2RQ.

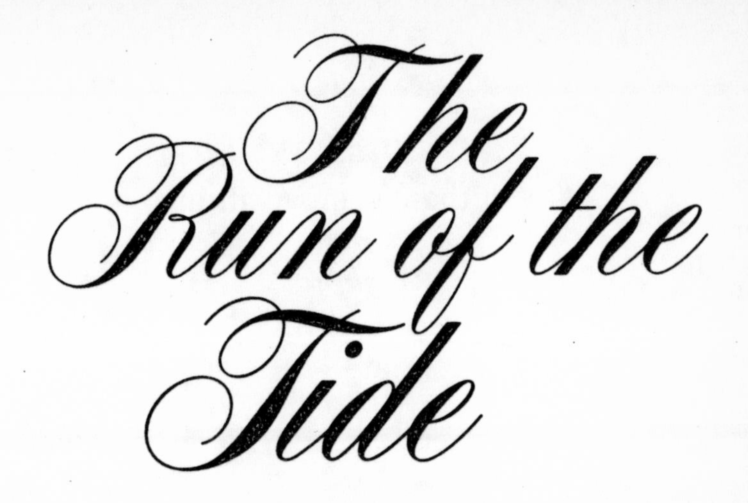

Forty years of coastal and Channel cruising in wooden boats

C. W. R. WINTER

Foreword by Sir Alec Rose

Patrick Stephens Limited

Dedication

To all those who sailed in:
Merlin
Grayling
Peradventure
and
Narija

First published in 1990

British Library Cataloguing in Publication Data

Winter, Ron
The run of the tide: 40 years of coastal and Channel cruising in wooden boats.
1. Great Britain. Sailing, ca. 1930-1978
I. Title II. Winter, Pat
797.1'24'0941

ISBN 1-85260-260-0

Patrick Stephens Limited is part of the Thorsons Publishing Group, Wellingborough, Northamptonshire NN8 2RQ, England.

Typeset by Harper Phototypesetters Limited, Northampton, England
Printed in Great Britain by William Collins Sons & Co. Ltd, Glasgow

1 3 5 7 9 10 8 6 4 2

Contents

List of Charts

The charts should be studied together with the text as they cover all the voyages described.

Acknowledgements

With one exception all the drawings and charts were made by Anthony Winter who knows the area better than any of us. The exception is the one on page 68 which is of Queenborough, Isle of Sheppey, sketched from Merlin's cockpit by Geoff Hartley.

All the photographs have been collected and arranged by my wife, Pat Winter. Many of them are her own work.

Foreword

by Sir Alec Rose KB

I AM very happy to write this Foreword to this collection of short stories — for this is what they are — of the adventures of the author cruising the creeks and inlets of the Essex, North Kent and Channel coasts over a period of forty years or so.

It made me reminisce back to my early years of sailing, when one could sail into a harbour or river inlet, anchor, be welcomed by the locals and spend the night in peace and solitude.

The author tells of his navigational triumphs in feeling his way into a muddy inlet and with equal candour his mistakes when finding himself aground. One can only admire his dedication to sailing, his good seamanship and what shines through to all good sailors — his love for his yacht.

A book for the armchair sailor's bookshelf, to be picked up and read as one feels the urge of owning your own boat.

Introduction

THE *Run of the Tide* is a collection of stories about sailing. All are the personal experiences of the author, and cover almost forty years of sailing and cruising yachts on the south and east coasts of England, and the coasts of France and Belgium. They describe cruises made in four different boats owned by the author, and accompanied by his family or by various friends, and they include a reference to his floating home, the Thames sailing barge *Magnet* on the busy Medway River in Rochester. All the boats written about were old ones, all were built of wood, but all were thoroughbreds, guaranteed to endear themselves to those who sailed in them.

The first one was *Merlin*, a 7-ton Bermudan cutter, built on the Essex coast in the early years of this century, and registered in the Port of Maldon. In her the author and his family learned many lessons in and around the Thames Estuary, and first savoured the delights and satisfactions of 'going foreign'. The second boat, *Grayling* was really a gentleman's yacht, with a mahogany-panelled saloon, and a draft of 6ft 9in. The latter brought her into contact many times with the Essex mud, but was partly responsible for giving her exceptional sailing qualities, and a fair turn of speed.

The third one was, again, a 7-tonner, but one with a distinguished pedigree. She was *Peradventure*, a Harrison-Butler design built by Anderson Rigden and Perkins of Whitstable for the late Ewan Montague who was Recorder for Middlesex. For many years *Peradventure* had a mooring in the Beaulieu River from which it was possible to explore and relish the delights of the Solent area.

The fourth boat was perhaps the most aristocratic of them all, the 14-ton John Bain-designed, Silver-built, motor yacht *Narija*, and in her it was possible to cruise in a greater degree of comfort.

The Run of the Tide does not chronicle any heroic voyages, such as round the world, or across the Atlantic. It is entirely confined to 'messing about in boats' in and out of the creeks and harbours of southern England

and the Channel and it is written for those many others who are interested in doing just that, and particularly for those who love and appreciate the character of old wooden cruising boats.

Ron Winter
Isle of Wight

The Anchorage

The anchorage is full of gentle sounds,
And hot sun makes the bright work warm to the touch.
The burgee barely ruffles in the morning breeze,
And as the Skipper rows ashore
The hollow roll of the rowlocks is soft and satisfying to the ear.
Then life is good, and a ship the only sensible communion
With sea and sky.

Such days are few, and therefore specially blest,
For grey days come, and dark clouds march
In never ending ranks across the sky.
The wind bites, and salt is in the air and on the tongue.
Shrouds brace bravely to the strain,
And sing their challenge to the wind.
My heart sings too, and lifts with the surge of the ship
To every combing wave.

The distant mooring nears, the seas are stilled,
A sudden burst of energy on deck
Rounds up, hands sails, and deftly plucks the buoy.
Sails are stowed, sheets coiled, and riding light secured,
And through the open hatch the lamplight gleams,
As bacon sizzles gently in the pan.

This is the greatest moment, release from toil,
Lotus land, the Song of Simeon, Chaminade's Autumn.
While ships swing slowly and silently at their moorings.

Ron Winter

PART 1

MERLIN

O to sail in a ship!
To leave this steady unendurable land,
To leave the tiresome sameness of the streets, the sidewalks and the houses,
To leave you O you solid motionless land, and entering a ship,
To sail and sail and sail!

WALT WHITMAN

1

An introduction to magic

SOME people change their boats as frequently as they change their cars, but no matter how many, nor how splendid some of these boats may be, your first boat always occupies a particular place in your affections, for in her and with her you discovered a new and magical world.

Merlin was my first boat, and the things that she and I discovered together still bring a glow of satisfaction to my heart, and occasionally a blush of shame to my cheek. Her vital statistics were simple and satisfying. Overall length 27 ft, waterline length 24 ft, beam 8 ft 6 in, and draught an incredible 5 ft 6 in. That last figure is engraved on my memory, for I learned all about going aground in *Merlin*.

She was built in the early years of this century by Messrs Barr and Pain of Leigh-on-Sea in Essex, and was registered in the Port of Maldon. As was perhaps to be expected her lines owed something to oyster smack design, with low freeboard aft, this latter feature enabling washing-up to be done

over the side from the cockpit with ease. It must be remembered that forty years ago the water round these islands was still comparatively clean and free of pollution. Despite her draught there was only sitting headroom down below, her underwater hull lines being very sleek, with a considerable fin keel. Her shape made her quite unsuitable for taking the ground as she lay over at an alarming angle.

Merlin had a longish bowsprit, a counter stern, and was cutter rigged. Originally she would have had a gaff main, but when I bought her in Gosport in 1949 her mainsail was Bermudan with quite a high aspect ratio. Standing rigging was uncomplicated and practical with shrouds adjusted by means of lanyards and dead-eyes — a very workmanlike arrangement. She had two very stout timber pin rails, port and starboard, which were most satisfactory, and in fact all her deck fittings were strong and seamanlike, as one would expect coming from an Essex yard. Her Thames Measurement tonnage was 7, and Register tonnage 3.71. Her cockpit was capacious and comfortable and as a first family boat she had much to commend her.

My introduction to sailing had taken place at the end of August 1939 when some friends invited me to sail with them on the Broads. After a couple of hours sailing up and down, during which time I had banged my head several times on the boom, cracked my funny bone on the cockpit coaming, and been generally uncomfortable, I was reluctantly persuaded to take the helm, and was left to my own devices. The revelation I then experienced rivalled that which met St Paul on the road to Damascus. The sun was shining and there was no noise other than that of the boat through the water, the peace was utter and complete.

After about twenty minutes it suddenly dawned on me that this was it. This was even better than ice-skating. This was what I had been waiting for all my life. And why had no one told me before now? Thinking of all the wasted years behind me I felt considerably aggrieved. For the rest of the afternoon my friends found it impossible to wrest the tiller from my grasp.

This experience convinced me that I must acquire a boat, and only the outbreak of war a week later prevented me from doing something about it right away. In fact, due to the war and its aftermath it was almost ten years later before I was able to make the dream a reality. In the interim I read everything I could lay my hands on, from Slocum to Francis B. Cooke, and consequently when the time to go boat hunting arrived I approached the problem with some idea of what to look for.

I shall never forget the day I met *Merlin*. She was advertised by the Hardway Yacht and Engineering Co Ltd, and though only the briefest particulars were given I travelled down to Gosport from my home in Sandwich to see her. It was a glorious day and as the owner of the yard rowed me out to her I could not believe my eyes. She was far more beautiful than I had imagined and I stepped aboard in a bit of a daze. He left me there for half an hour so that there was plenty of time to check the long list of things I had brought with me, but I was already so much in love that many of them were forgotten. At this distance I can only remember fingering the shroud lanyards and sitting on one of the settee berths with the sunlight streaming in through the hatch and the water lapping lazily against her hull as she rocked gently on her mooring. When my friend returned it was very difficult not to appear too eager to buy her, for the compulsion to own this beautiful and graceful creature was overwhelming.

As soon as she was mine an introduction took me to Portsmouth to see Harry Feltham, at that time an old man and a legendary figure in the boating world. I asked him to look her over and give me his opinion without going to the expense of a full survey.

'I know what you want' he said, 'You want me to tell you whether she will drown you or not'.

And this was exactly it. When I went back a week later he said:

'She has been laid up afloat all through the war and is in rough condition, but she won't drown you'. He smiled and added 'I reckon she will outlive you!'

A friend from the Little Ship Club offered to risk his life helping to sail *Merlin* round to Sandwich, and this was gratefully accepted. Stanley Swan had served during the war in armed trawlers and was truly an intrepid mariner, with a vast experience in sailing all sorts of small boats. It is possible that I had more sea miles to my credit than he, for my time had been served in one of the greatest ships of all, the *Queen Mary*, but there is no doubt that in courage and experience of small craft he was way ahead, and his help was invaluable.

The voyage from Gosport to Sandwich was planned to be completed in one weekend, but in the event we ran into a bit of a blow off Rottingdean and had the misfortune to lose the dinghy, which we were towing. As a result we put into Newhaven and left her there for the week.

The following weekend our departure from Newhaven was delayed while I retrieved the dinghy which had blown ashore further along the coast, and we then found ourselves becalmed off Dungeness for several hours. The smart breeze that followed this calm came from the north-east, which made weathering the Foreland difficult, and in making a long leg out into the Channel we ran into a rather lumpy sea. *Merlin* bounced about a bit and gave us a most exhilarating ride, but happening to look down the hatch I was horrified to find the cabin half full of water. This was soon pumped out but we had obviously sprung a leak, and this got steadily worse until I was pumping almost continuously.

Discretion being the better part of valour we took her into Dover and the following day I had her lifted out of the water. The trouble was readily located and cured — a scarf joint in her forefoot had opened up, the result of seven years' lack of maintenance — and while she was out of the water the opportunity was taken to renew some of the caulking which was also looking rather sorry for itself.

This initial cruise, however, confirmed my first impressions of *Merlin*, and I was delighted with her speed, her performance on the wind, and her ease of handling. It was gratifying to find that my wife and our two small children also endorsed this opinion and rapidly became attached to her. As indeed did our dog, a mongrel Welsh sheepdog called Mac, who took to sailing with an enthusiasm comical to behold. Mac was always first into the dinghy when we went out in her, and the last and most reluctant to come ashore.

Of course there were problems. The Sandwich Stour was not a suitable river for a boat of this draft, and it became our practice to get out to sea each weekend on the first available tide and make neighbouring Ramsgate our headquarters. It must be said that we did not always make it, the river wound a tortuous course across the mud flats of Pegwell Bay, and there were occasions in the half light of early dawn when we missed a bend and spent a few hours waiting for the tide to return.

Another problem was the engine, which was a 2 hp air-cooled Norman. This was a very simple piece of machinery which after a complete overhaul (carried out in the calm off Dungeness) worked perfectly, but which was quite inadequate in power for a boat of *Merlin*'s size.

But despite the problems *Merlin* was a huge success. She introduced us, all five of us (Mac being the fifth), to a new and magical world of sailing, to aspects of the open-air life we had never previously experienced, and she gave us a hobby which became a life-long passion.

When you buy your first boat, having had little experience of sailing, the new world that opens up is certainly magical and exciting, but it is also a very practical world. There is so much to be learned, and many of the lessons are accompanied by cold and wet conditions, and occasionally by fear. But there is nothing like a little honest fright to get the adrenalin

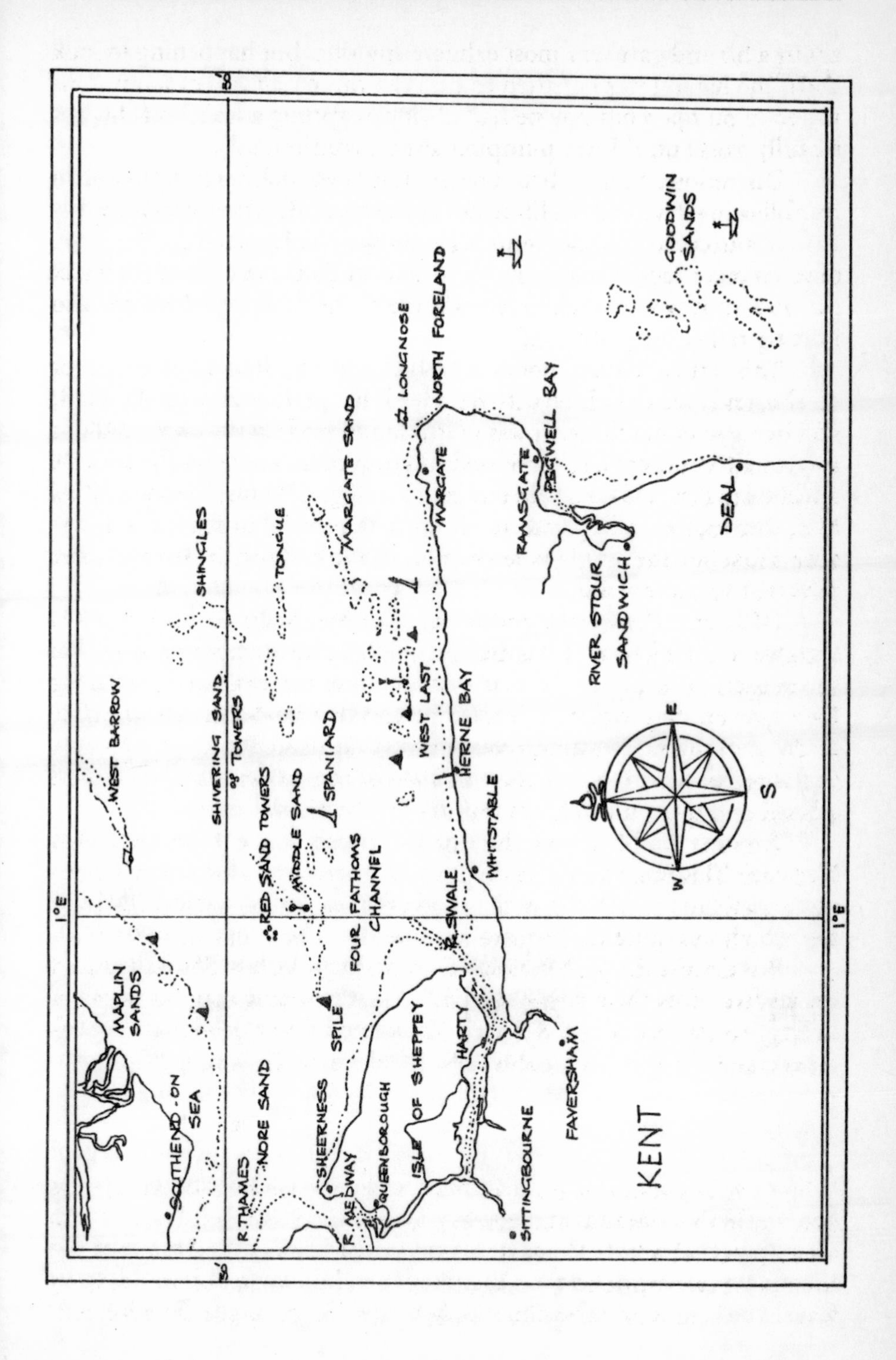
SOUTHEND-ON SEA
MAPLIN SANDS
WEST BARROW
SHIVERING SAND
of TOWERS
SHINGLES
R. THAMES
NORE SAND
SPILE
RED SAND TOWERS
MIDDLE SAND
SPANIARD
TONGUE
MARGATE SAND
LONGNOSE
SHEERNESS
FOUR FATHOMS CHANNEL
WEST LAST
R. MEDWAY
QUEENBOROUGH
ISLE OF SHEPPEY
HARTY
R. SWALE
WHITSTABLE
HERNE BAY
MARGATE
NORTH FORELAND
RAMSGATE
PEGWELL BAY
SITTINGBOURNE
FAVERSHAM
KENT
RIVER STOUR
SANDWICH
DEAL
GOODWIN SANDS
W
E
S
1°E
50'

running. And of course the rewards are enormous. To overcome the cold and wet, and any other unpleasantness the sea can produce, and to arrive at one's planned destination safely — particularly if this is a foreign one — brings a glow of success that is hard to beat.

With *Merlin* my family and I were really starting from scratch, learning from first principles, and in our first season we probably made more mistakes than most. As soon as possible I enrolled for courses in seamanship and navigation at the Little Ship Club, and these proved to be absolutely invaluable. Gradually our flounderings around off the north Kent coast became a little less uncontrolled and ultimately we achieved a measure of efficiency of which I was modestly proud.

After one small hiccough the children took to all this with great enthusiasm and rapidly became proficient members of the crew. Anthony was ten at the time, and Sally eight, but they both worked hard, learning their knots, helping with sail setting, getting fenders in and out, looking after the dinghy, etc. The hiccough referred to occurred the first time we took them out in *Merlin*. They were both wildly excited at the prospect, but were not prepared for what happened. It was a bit choppy and they were both seasick, and were not in the least bit amused. 'You never told us it would be like this!' they complained. We returned home and they recovered, but the thought that they were not going to like sailing was rather depressing. After all, we had just spent all our savings on buying the boat. The next morning breakfast was a rather thoughtful meal, until Anthony suddenly perked up and said 'Well come on, what time are we going sailing?' From then on they never looked back.

Perhaps the first lesson I learned, and one that was quickly passed on to the children, was the old dictum 'one hand for the ship and one for yourself'. This was before the days of guard rails, life jackets and life lines, and you were expected to look after yourself. The dangers of not doing so were brought home to us one day in dramatic fashion, and the lesson we learned was salutory. It happened this way.

One Sunday morning we left Ramsgate harbour for a sail. We had been moored between two other boats and had had to extricate ourselves stern first. Sally had been given the job of looking after the dinghy to see that it did not get trapped, and when we were clear she had to make the painter fast again. This she was perfectly capable of doing, and was good at knots, but she regarded the dinghy as her own personal property and took rather a long time doing it.

Outside the breeze was fresh and from astern, and *Merlin* began to tramp along. My wife was on the tiller and Anthony and I went forward to set the staysail. And then we gybed. My wife shouted 'Gybe-O!' and

I turned round in time to see Sally and Mac, the dog, standing on the counter as the boom came across and swept her into the drink. Mac got entangled in the main sheet and for a moment was all fur and feathers, and looked as if he was going over too.

As luck would have it Sally had tied the dinghy up at the full extent of its painter, which was a long one, and as her head broke water the dinghy was just passing her. As cool as a cucumber she reached up and grasped the gunwale. My wife, who was a very strong swimmer, desisted from the plunge she was about to take, and I hauled the dinghy up to the counter and jumped in.

In no time at all we had Sally back aboard by which time my anxiety was turning to anger, but before I could say anything she disarmed criticism by saying 'I'm not going to blame anybody — it was my own fault!'

The lessons to be learned from this seemed obvious: Always wear a life jacket at sea, don't stand about where there is nothing to hold on to, and — a special lesson for me — keep a closer watch on the kids. This accident certainly made some of us more careful. As a result of it I bought Sally a little silver St Christopher pendant for being brave, and visited my old friend Captain Watts for two childrens' life jackets.

These were worn with great enthusiasm the following weekend, and it was with great difficulty that we dissuaded Anthony from jumping overboard to see if they really did work. Sally too tended to become deliberately careless, and in the end we decided they were actually safer without them. This may shock present day pundits in this safety-conscious age, but I report only the simple truth, and it is a fact that the children both learned to look after themselves and grew up to be responsible sailors and caring parents.

Merlin was normally moored alongside an old wharf in the River Stour in Sandwich. This used to dry out on the tide and so she was a constant source of anxiety, not only to me but to the Harbour Master, who made no bones about his dislike of her. The river was not only shallow but narrow, and wound its way out to sea across extensive mud flats. It is true the channel was buoyed, since Thames barges were trading into Sandwich with timber at this time, but in order to get our sailing in at the weekend we frequently had to leave before daybreak and the buoys were difficult to see in the dark.

We did not go aground very often, but when we did *Merlin* would lie down at a very uncomfortable angle and we would have to abandon ship. The first time this happened I was worried lest she should fill before floating on the rising tide, and as a precaution decided to off-load all the internal ballast of which there was almost half a ton. Most of this I was able to row ashore in the dinghy before the water left us, but it was a slow, painstaking, and exceedingly dirty business, and as it turned out, quite unnecessary.

It was also a waste of time and effort to build up the side of the cockpit with the floorboards, for when the tide returned she lifted without trouble. So apart from losing a day's sailing and having to restow the ballast and clean up a very dirty ship, we were none the worse for the experience. And one of us at least, was a little wiser.

Each weekend on coming out from Sandwich river we made for Ramsgate, where we knew we could get in and out at any state of the tide, and we learned a lot in this harbour entrance which is narrow and subject to great variations in tidal flow. On a spring ebb Ramsgate is rather like Yarmouth in the Isle of Wight, for in both places the tide sluices across the entrance at about 4 knots, and *Merlin*'s little 2 hp engine was barely able to stem this. As it was we just managed to creep in crabwise with her bowsprit pointing firmly at one of the pier-heads.

During our first summer afloat we practised our seamanship assiduously. We tried picking up a mooring under sail in different states of wind and tide, and also coming alongside and getting away. We found this was a bit like learning to ride a bicycle, for a long time it seemed hopeless, and then suddenly you found you could judge the speed of the ship and how she was going to handle. My own confidence had a boost fairly early on when we passed a shrimping boat off Whitstable and I was able to turn *Merlin* round, catch the shrimper up, and hover alongside while my wife negotiated the purchase of our tea.

We also acquired the almost instinctive feel for the position of the wind, and the ability to find the best setting for the headsails and the main sheet. We learned that 'pinching' her when on the wind is just not sensible, it being far better to keep her moving as fast as possible, even though this means she is not pointing quite as high as you think she ought. And of course we practiced going about over and over again, and learned how to shoot up into the eye of the wind, an operation which the children particularly enjoyed.

Another lesson which the children had to learn was not to laugh at the discomforture of others who might be making a mess of things. This arose out of an embarrassing incident in Stangate Creek, a delightful anchorage we frequented in the Medway, which was used by a variety of Naval craft. One afternoon a very smart and fast Naval launch came roaring up to pick up a buoy we were just passing. A sailor was stationed in the bows with his boathook at the ready, and the intention was clearly to stop the boat precisely at the buoy to enable the sailor to pick it up smartly: he had obviously learned this by numbers as a drill.

The launch came charging up at a rate of knots, and then went full speed astern in order to bring it to a standstill exactly at the buoy in a welter of white water. Unfortunately the man on the throttles misjudged it by about a yard and the poor sailor on the bow went through all the motions smartly with his boathook, but could only pick up air and very nearly went base over apex into the drink to boot. Up to this point the children had been most impressed with this exhibition of boat handling and naval discipline, but when the poor bowman overbalanced they burst out laughing and we thought Sally particularly was going to do herself a mischief. It was especially embarrassing as the helmsman of the launch had switched off his engines and had to start all over again. We crept silently away as fast as our sails would carry us, feeling strangely comforted that even the Royal Navy sometimes got things wrong.

But the Navy had the last laugh. That night we picked up a mooring buoy in a small inlet off Stangate Creek and were very snug. There was no one else about and we were protected from what wind there was by the marshes on each side. But at 2.30 am. I received a loud hail, and a strong searchlight was shone on us. Yes, it was a naval mooring we had picked up, and though they did not want to use it themselves they equally did not wish us to have it, and we had to move.

2

Deeper waters

THERE was no doubt about it, *Merlin*'s little 2 hp air-cooled engine had to go. This decision was taken reluctantly as the engine was a very simple and uncomplicated piece of machinery, easy to maintain and to start, and reliable in performance. But it was just not man enough for the job.

It would have been nice to have installed a brand new larger engine, but the cost seemed prohibitive, though with hindsight, and greater experience, an 8 hp. Stuart Turner would have been ideal for this boat, and a good investment. Just at this time however I came under the influence of a young friend, Derek, who worked for a local firm of agricultural engineers in Sandwich, and who was a willing and eager learner in this new world of sailing. Derek persuaded me of the feasibility, and indeed the desirability, of purchasing two scrap Austin 7 engines that were lying about in the yard, and producing from them one reconditioned, as-good-as-new, marinized engine.

Derek taught me a lot, including how to grind in valves by hand, a long and painful process, and in due course we achieved our object and mounted the engine in the boat. Alas, it was never 100% satisfactory. To

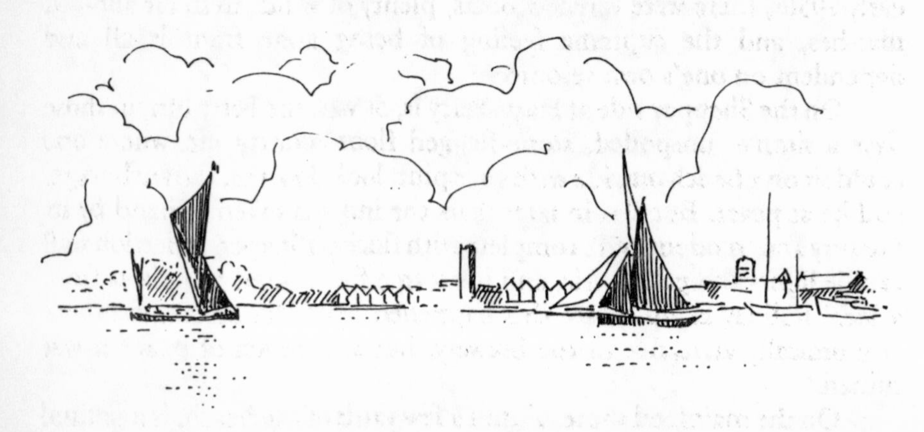

begin with the Austin engine was basically built of aluminium, and this did not take kindly to the salt sea water that was pumped round it for cooling purposes. Secondly, and this was equally important, the engine took up much more room than the 2 hp Norman, and space below the cockpit was at a premium, the net result being that it was impossible to mount it in a straight line with the propellor shaft. This meant driving the shaft through a flexible coupling, and though the angle was relatively small this coupling was a constant source of trouble and always seemed to fail at the most crucial moments.

From this we learned that the two essential requirements of an auxiliary marine engine are instant starting — for though you may not need the engine very often, when you do you usually need it urgently — and reliability, that is, the ability to keep plugging away hour after hour, so that even though the weather has turned sour and the tide is foul you can have confidence that she will in due course get you home.

With the new engine, though, we certainly had more power, and the terrors of beating against the tide were somewhat diminished. We still of course had the problem of getting out of Sandwich River in the dark and negotiating the many bends in the channel, and on one ghastly occasion I mistook a port hand for a starboard hand buoy, went the wrong side of it, went aground, and, not realizing what I had done wrong, got into the dinghy and actually towed *Merlin* another 40 ft further on to the mud! On a falling tide.

But the good times far outweighed the bad, and as our experience increased, so did our enjoyment. A favourite short cruise from Ramsgate was round the North Foreland and along the north Kent coast past Margate, Herne Bay, and Whitstable to the Isle of Sheppey and the River Swale where there is a delightful anchorage at Harty Ferry. Here, in the early 1950s, there were very few boats, plenty of wind, fresh air and salt marshes, and the supreme feeling of being away from it all and dependent on one's own resources.

On the Sheppey side at Harty Ferry is, or was, the Ferry Inn, in those days a simple, unspoiled, stone-flagged floor country inn where one could sit on a bench outside with your pint, look down on the anchorage, and be at peace. But alas in later years the inn was taken in hand by its brewery and 'modernized', complete with flock wallpaper, imitation wall candle lights and pop music, and it became frequented by visitors from a local holiday camp. Once this happened it no doubt became more economically attractive to the brewery, but as a haven of peace it was ruined.

On the mainland shore, within a few yards of the beach, is a natural spring producing gallons of beautiful ice-cold drinking water per minute, a spring that works incessantly and never seems to fail. Altogether Harty Ferry was ideal for the family yachtsman who wanted peace and quiet, and what made it even more complete was that a few hundred yards downstream, perhaps half a mile or so, was a short stretch of sandy beach that was almost inaccessible from the land. To this we would sail in the morning, anchor a few yards off, and go ashore in the dinghy. Here the children — and Mac — could play to their hearts content, either on the beach, or in the dinghy, or in *Merlin*. It was as good as having our own uninhabited island.

To find one's way to Harty Ferry from Ramsgate was not difficult, but it did afford the opportunity to practice a little navigation, both by

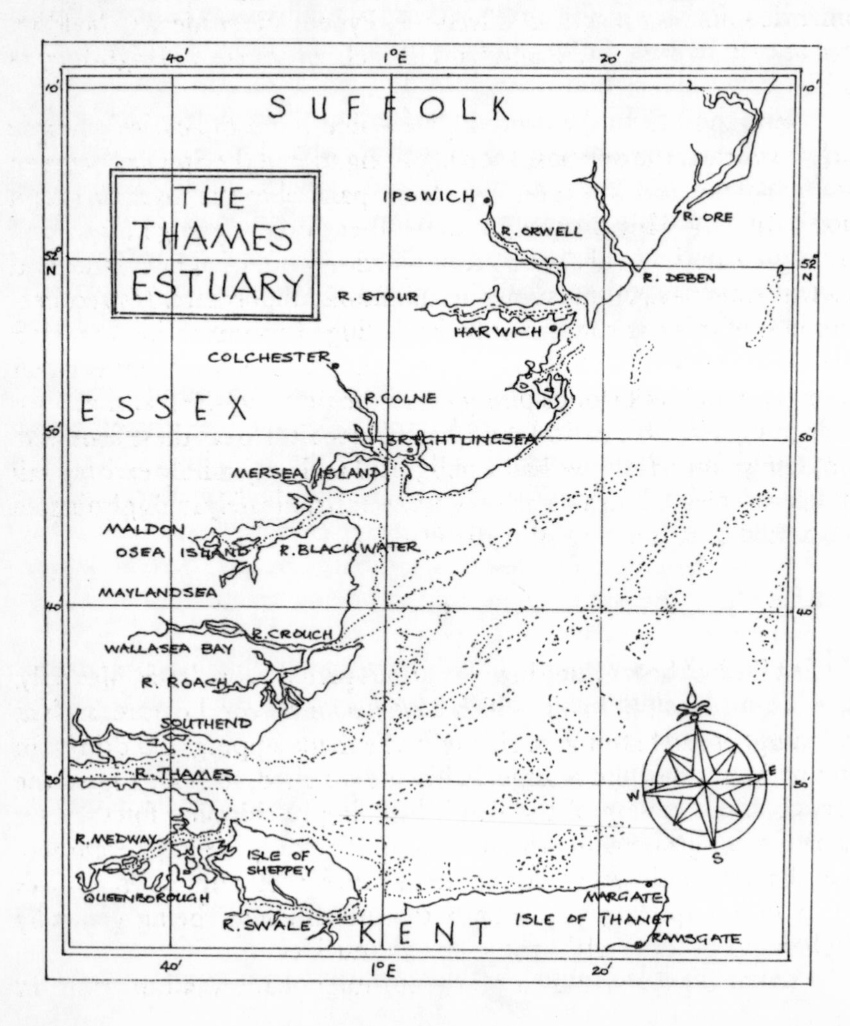

compass and by 'buoy hopping'. And this was good preparation for the next step, which was to cross the Thames estuary to the Essex coast. It seemed a terribly venturesome step at the time and brought home to the Skipper the responsibility he carried, both for the safety of the ship and the lives of those aboard.

Actually the first crossing we ever made started from Queenborough at the other end of the River Swale which divides Sheppey from the mainland. Our target was Brightlingsea, an ancient fishing port on the River Colne that we had long wanted to visit, and which was a good centre for exploring the Colne and Blackwater rivers and even the other Essex rivers, Crouch and Roach. This was a fascinating area that through the war years we had read much about, and we were eager to discover such romantic sounding places as Wivenhoe, Pyfleet, West Mersea, Maldon, Bradwell, Burnham, and Paglesham, as well, of course, as Brightlingsea itself.

Navigation from the Swale to the Colne was comparatively simple in clear weather, the one possible snag being to find the Spitway between the Buxey and Gunfleet sands which ran parallel to the Essex coast and barred the way. This channel, marked at each end by large buoys and carrying a least depth of about 5 ft, is practically out of sight of land, and to a first time navigator assumes an unnatural importance. My recollections now of this trip concern only the feeling of apprehension as we left Queenborough around 4.30 am, and as we approached the Gunfleet later on the sight of black clouds piling up to the west and the fear that I was never going to be able to find the Spitway. Needless to say these fears were completely groundless: we had a delightful and only mildly exciting sail but felt very pleased with ourselves when we arrived safely in Brightlingsea and picked up a mooring near the Hard.

★ ★ ★

The first flush of boat ownership is a curious period in one's life. Mentally, there is a shedding of habits which have become second nature, such as gardening, or sun bathing, or sitting in the shade sipping cold drinks. In place of these, other and stranger habits are acquired, such as gauging the strength and direction of the wind, listening to shipping forecasts, or practicing tying a bowline with one hand. Physically life is different too, for one is frequently wet and often tired, with hitherto unknown muscles aching in a surprising way. Hands too are different, being generally rougher and swollen, with many grazed knuckles.

But the biggest change is on the spiritual plane, as all the time, in all one's waking hours, there is a tremendous feeling of elation, a bubbling up of suppressed excitement, the sort of feeling that makes even non-singers burst into song. For life in all its aspects has indeed changed, and the knowledge of this, and the realization that new adventures, new thrills, and new worlds lie ahead, causes the pulse to quicken and the heart to beat a little faster.

Being a wage slave my sailing had perforce to be carried out at the weekend, but all through the working week in my office in the heart of London, it was possible occasionally to look out of the window and see the scudding clouds, and wonder whether perhaps the jib sheet might not be hardened in a little to make her point a little higher.

At the weekend daydreams suddenly became reality and we were off again. It did not seem to matter much what the weather was doing, for even if it was too bad actually to sail there was always plenty to do, plans to be made, ropes spliced, ends whipped. It was all fascinating and absorbing and the weekends passed all too quickly.

The sailing season itself simply flew past, and though we resented the approach of winter we planned a programme of work for the lay-up period which would give us all something to do and remind us of the days to come. Due to her long lay-up during the war *Merlin* was not in good condition when we bought her, and after our first idyllic sailing season we planned to give her a pretty thorough overhaul. Naturally the hardest of the hard work devolved on me, and also on our young friend Derek, who turned out to be a fanatical enthusiast to whom no problem was insuperable.

Below the town of Sandwich the river Stour meanders across the marshes for a couple of miles to the sea, passing through a wild and desolate area across which the wind, when the weather is easterly, blows mercilessly from the sea. In the winter the temperature on the saltings is Siberian. Sandwich was once a major seaport, and indeed the premier port in England for embarkation to the continent, a port well known to the Romans, the Saxons, the Normans, and all our medieval English monarchs. But the sea has long since deserted the town, leaving this waste of marshes through which the river finds its way.

Outside the town are the remains of the Roman fort of *Rutupiae*, now Richborough, a massive and mysterious flint ruin from which led one of the first of all Roman roads in Britain, Watling Street. Also in this area lie the derelict remnants of the First World War port of Richborough, which was constructed to feed our armies in France. Many of the buildings have now been restored or rebuilt and a thriving industrial estate has developed, but at the time of which I write the National Coal Board owned a large part of this area with many empty and forlorn warehouses and a long length of wharf.

On this deserted wharf the Coal Board readily gave me permission to lay-up *Merlin*, and Derek and I set about the task of organizing the project. We spent the whole of one Saturday on the marshes collecting driftwood suitable for building a cradle, and I for one was astonished with what we found. Our haul included several railway sleepers in first class condition, and enough long lengths of heavy timber to have built half a dozen cradles had we wished. And all this within a quarter of a mile of the river bank.

All the timber we wanted we carried or dragged to the river and at low water lashed it together and launched it across the mud. Never have I seen such soft and glutinous mud as we encountered that day, never before or since have I so frequently been bogged down and lost a Wellington boot, never have I seen two such plastered creatures as Derek and I. But the operation was completed, and as the tide made we climbed into the dinghy and towed our unwieldly raft slowly up the river to the Coal Board wharf.

The building of the cradle was Derek's prerogative, and though the finished article was not a thing of beauty, it was solid and it was satisfactory. As soon as it was ready for occupation I hired a mobile crane, and at the top of the tide brought *Merlin* up to the wharf. The mast was no problem to unstep and we laid this on trestles out of the way. Then with slings and spreaders that we had manufactured we tackled the hull, and in no time at all *Merlin* was out of the water and after swaying gently to and fro for a few minutes was lowered slowly into her cradle which she fitted perfectly. This was a great tribute to Derek's skill, as he had not previously seen *Merlin* out of the water and had had to base his design on my rather ineffectual description and sketches of her hull shape.

So there she sat, exposed to all the winds that blew from the east or north, but safe and sound. And then began the really hard work, scraping her down to bare wood, and though Derek helped with this it was only right that I should do the major share. Weekend after weekend I trundled on my bicycle the mile or so down the road from Sandwich to the wharf, and scraped, and scraped, and scraped. What I found under the paint was encouraging. *Merlin* was built of pitch pine, and with the exception of teak this is the finest wood for boat construction. And the wood of *Merlin*'s hull was really in good shape. Only the caulking left something to be desired: in places this was certainly rather old and tired, and simply had to be renewed.

And so the winter wore on, and gradually the work was done. When it rained I rigged up a partial shelter with a tarpaulin, but when the wind blew I really suffered. At times the cold was so intense that it was quite impossible to work, but we acquired an old 50 gallon oil drum, punched a few holes in it, and kept a roaring fire going. There was plenty of wood on the marshes, and it was astonishing what a difference a bit of fire made, not only to my numbed fingers but also to my morale.

By the time Easter came round she was ready. Her topsides had been primed, undercoated, and glossed, her bottom painted and anti-fouled. All the rigging had been examined, and renewed where necessary. The ash blocks had been scraped down and re-varnished, and gleamed as when new. The dinghy too had been refurbished and this had proved to be one of the most fiddling jobs of all since this was a clinker-built boat, and varnished. There is nothing more tedious than scraping out all the internal corners in a small clinker-built boat, but ultimately this task too was completed, and the dinghy together with *Merlin* herself was once again 'in all respects ready for sea' and another summer of cruising. This year we were to spread our wings a little and achieve an ambition that had been growing steadily, the ambition to 'go foreign'.

3

Cruising and foreign travel

THE north and east coasts of Kent may not be among the most picturesque cruising areas for small yachts — they hardly compare with the Solent or with the Essex or Suffolk rivers — but they are splendid coasts on which to learn. At the time of which I write both Ramsgate and Dover welcomed yachtsmen, and had entrances that were not too difficult to negotiate, and further west the Medway estuary was a delight. In between were the channels and shoals of the Thames estuary and the River Swale which provided plenty of navigational practice for a boat drawing over 5 ft.

Though the Sandwich River was only navigable on the tide Ramsgate was conveniently near and was an excellent centre for exploring westwards to the Medway, northwards across the Thames estuary to Essex, and southwards to Dover and the continent. As experience and confidence grew so did our cruising boundaries, and though we never attempted anything heroic *Merlin* took us on many modest and interesting cruises. Another development brought about by increasing confidence was a desire to share the fun we were having with friends, and *Merlin* was frequently loaded to capacity, and sometimes beyond.

The first time foreign is always a milestone, and on this occasion we had to leave Mac behind, much to his disgust and distress. We were late leaving and missed the best of the tide, and by the time we had passed Deal on our way to Dover the tide began to turn. As evening approached the wind fell light and we were soon battling against a foul tide on a flat calm sea. The new engine was running well but I was worried about the flexible coupling in the drive which had already given signs of not liking the angle through which it had to work. Off Kingsgate we decided that enough was enough, dropped the anchor, piled into the dinghy and went ashore, where after a short bus ride we found a very pleasant restaurant.

When we came back *Merlin*'s nose was pointing to the north and we were soon on our way. The children were persuaded reluctantly to go to bed, though they did not sleep and we soon discovered they were taking an active interest in what was going on. This was their first night passage and they were understandably excited.

Night fell before we reached Dover, and approaching the eastern entrance to the port in the dark was great fun. We switched on our navigation lights when we were about 200 yards away from the entrance, and this was the signal for several things to happen, all of which brought forth excited shouts from the children. First to blaze into life were the red and green lights on the breakwater on either side of the entrance, these being the signal permitting us to enter. These were followed by a searchlight from the signal bridge which picked us up and had a very good look. Then, as we got a little nearer, a voice came over the loud hailer requesting that as soon as we entered we should alter course and sail in close to the signal bridge.

This we did and were hailed again in the same manner with the following questions: 'What is the name of your ship?' 'What is the master's name?' (Ribaldry from the children at this one.) 'Where are you from?' These answered we were free to proceed and find ourselves a berth. Entering the harbour in total darkness we felt our way into the Camber — the old Submarine Basin — where moorings for yachts were free, and dropped anchor. It was not long before we all had our heads down and were fast asleep.

Alas for the plans we made for an early start next morning! When we woke it was to find a gale blowing outside and *Merlin* rolling at her anchor, so that a day in harbour was obviously inevitable. By the following morning the wind had died completely again — though not the sea — but we decided to make a start, and hoped that we would pick up a breeze on the way. Consequently I hailed the Customs launch as it cruised round on its morning tour of inspection, and requested permission to leave. The launch slid slowly past us and the officer called out, 'Where are you bound?' 'Calais' He looked at me for a moment and then said 'OK Skipper — when you are ready.' And that was the conclusion of formalities.

Outside the harbour a swell was running and the tide began to set us strongly to the east, but it was a lovely day and we plugged on, the engine running sweetly. For two hours we progressed steadily and a light sou'westerly breeze filled our sails and helped us on our way.

And then it happened! Without any warning at all there was a horrible noise from under the cockpit grating, bits flew in all directions and the engine, suddenly relieved of its load, raced away. We all knew what had occurred; the coupling, tired of gyrating through an uncomfortable angle, had come adrift. We had a committee meeting and reluctantly decided that the prudent thing to do was to put back to Dover, so up went the helm and we gybed her round.

It took exactly an hour and a half to find all the pieces and re-assemble the coupling, and I secretly shared the crew's surprise on finding that it worked. In some trepidation we started the engine and threw her into gear, but after ten minutes of perfect performance confidence returned and we decided that perhaps it was going to hold after all.

By this time we were about a mile off Dover harbour, but the breeze had freshened considerably and we were making quite a good speed through the water. As the engine was now in working order and the conditions were just right there was absolutely no point in going back to England, so we put about without more ado and once again set course for the French coast. For the next four hours we had a truly wonderful sail. The wind freshened still more, the sun shone, and *Merlin* bounded along with all her canvas drawing.

As we got nearer the French coast we ran into a rather choppy sea and the dinghy began to occupy more and more of my attention. She had been trailing behind quite happily all the way across but now she began to sheer from side to side as we slid down each wave, and each time the towing painter jerked her back on course she shipped a little water. We tried hauling her up short but this was no use as she kept butting *Merlin*, and once or twice was in danger of getting trapped under the counter. As so very often happens on such occasions, we did not appreciate the seriousness of the situation until it was too late to do anything about it. As we turned to starboard to enter Calais harbour the dinghy sheered off and when the painter pulled taut she shipped a lot more water and rolled over. The painter immediately snapped and we had the mortifying experience of seeing our dinghy disappear astern — bottom up.

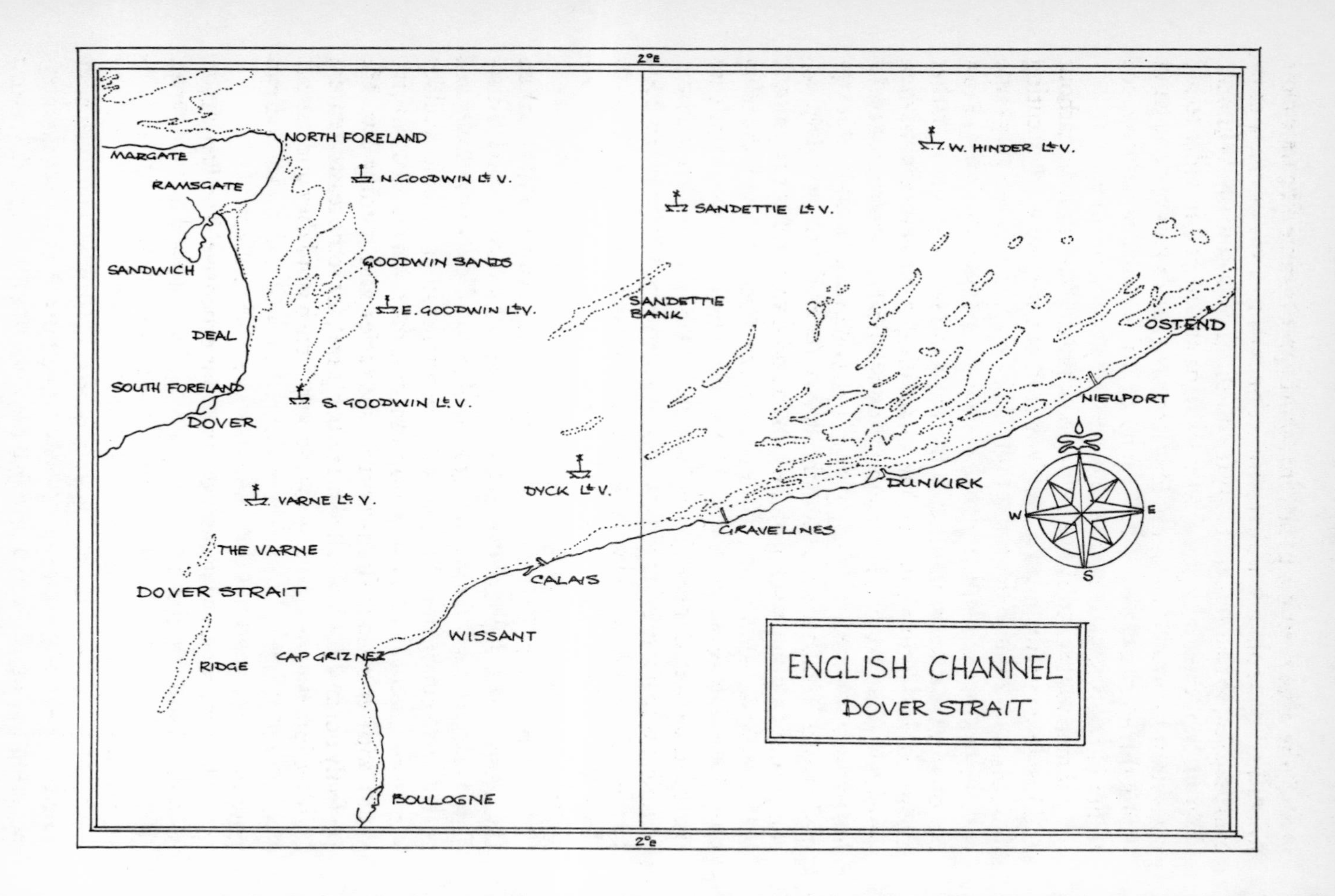
2°E
NORTH FORELAND
MARGATE
RAMSGATE
N. GOODWIN Lt V.
W. HINDER Lt V.
SANDETTIE Lt V.
SANDWICH
GOODWIN SANDS
SANDETTIE BANK
E. GOODWIN Lt V.
OSTEND
DEAL
SOUTH FORELAND
S. GOODWIN Lt V.
NIEUPORT
DOVER
DYCK Lt V.
DUNKIRK
VARNE Lt V.
W
E
S
GRAVELINES
THE VARNE
CALAIS
DOVER STRAIT
WISSANT
RIDGE
CAP GRIZ NEZ
ENGLISH CHANNEL
DOVER STRAIT
BOULOGNE
2°E

Quite a lot then happened in a short space of time. We were close to the harbour entrance with a strong tide setting across it and a nasty confused sea, so that we could only see the dinghy occasionally. While the children kept their eyes glued on it we went about, and in order to aid navigation I started the engine. This latter ran for about fifteen seconds before there was a repeat, on a larger scale, of the incident experienced earlier in the day, and the coupling flew to pieces once more.

Somebody then noticed a fishing boat putting out from the harbour and heading towards us, apparently to find out why we were executing these rather curious manoeuvres right in the entrance. When they came near we hailed them in our best French and explained that we had lost our dinghy. This was a bit tricky as the wind and sea were making rather a noise, and we didn't know the French for dinghy. However the children were highly diverted by their parents' first practical demonstration of the intricacies of the French language, and later gave us top marks for this top-of-the-voice explanation about the '*petit bateau*' that was lost, accompanied by much waving of the broken and frayed end of the painter.

Curiously enough the fishermen understood us, and shouting something completely unintelligible they proceeded out to sea while we turned and entered the harbour. Twenty minutes later they arrived back complete with the missing dinghy. By this time we had dropped our hook by the lifeboat station and were beginning to clean ship. The fishing boat came alongside, and after the exchange of the usual pleasantries, bargaining began.

For the French Republic there appeared three rather oddly assorted characters. The skipper of the fishing boat was a fat man dressed in dirty light blue jeans and three days' growth of beard. His eye was crafty and his accent incomprehensible. The other two were father and son, the elder a little wizened old fellow with no teeth, and the son a studious looking youth with enormous horn-rimmed spectacles and a trilby hat. His perfectly normal habit of called his father '*pere*', for some reason sent the children into fits — perhaps it was the only French word they understood. The United Kingdom was represented by my wife and myself and two goggle-eyed kids who were having the time of their lives.

The next fifteen minutes were fun, but expensive. The Frenchmen started at 7,000 francs and were prepared to come down, while we opened with an offer of 500 francs and were equally willing to go up. We ultimately met at 3,000 francs, which satisfied all parties, and to clinch the deal I asked Anthony to offer them a cigarette. These were fetched from below and he held out the packet to the skipper. The latter misunderstood the gesture as, with a gratified cry, he took the lot, and if Anthony had not stepped back smartly would, I think, have embraced him with typical Gallic enthusiasm.

As it was, we parted with handshakes all round and they insisted on towing us to another part of the harbour where they said we should be more comfortable. After all this we suddenly realized that we were very tired, so refusing a request for shore leave from the junior members of the crew, we had a meal and turned in, when in spite of *Merlin*'s incessant rolling we slept like logs.

★ ★ ★

Our first expedition abroad had not started all that well, as we arrived in Calais with a broken engine coupling and having had to pay 3,000 francs for the recovery of the dinghy which had gone missing as we entered the port. However, after a good night's sleep we all felt better able to cope with whatever fresh problems the day might bring.

An examination of the wreckage under the cockpit grating showed that a new coupling was going to be needed since the fabric centre of the old one was badly torn. So, with a highly excited section of the crew, we piled into the dinghy and rowed ashore.

Our first call was on the British Consul to enlist his aid in getting the coupling repaired, and his French secretary put us on to one Marcel Williaume who had a garage in the Rue de Vie. Marcel was a gem. Without a word of English at his command he listened with incredible gravity to our story, and after he and I had spent some time on his garage floor with a piece of chalk he announced himself willing to accept the assignment, and solemnly undertook, as a man of honour to repair the coupling to our complete satisfaction — or bust.

He was as good as his word too, and overcoming the difficulties in obtaining the necessary spare parts he made a darn good job of the repair so that from that day on we never had another moment's trouble with the coupling.

We emerged from his rather gloomy garage feeling rather depressed as we were faced with a miscarriage of all our plans for sailing along the coast. But as things turned out we need not have worried. The whole town was on holiday for the Festival of August 15th, and we could not have had a more entertaining time. The weather was perfect, and every day brought a new and interesting experience, not the least of the pleasure which my wife and I derived being the obvious enjoyment that the children were getting out of it.

There was the Miners' Band which paraded through the town, its members perspiring freely in their too-tight uniforms, and blowing themselves purple in the face. There was the beach with its fine sands and gay tents where we spent several hours lazing away, and where the only sad note was the pathetic groups of orphan children, a horrible reminder of the war. There was the first time Sally went into a public building labelled '*Dames*'. She came out of it in approximately six seconds and her face spoke volumes. She hadn't believed it possible. There were the children's first attempts at shopping, and the aplomb with which they bought themselves '*Glaces*' and (I regret to say) '*Frites*'. There was the first meal in a French restaurant and their reaction to lobster and wine. *Merlin*'s rolling did not worry them that night!

There was the duckling ceremony which was one of the highlights of the festival. Two men in a small boat rowed out to the middle of the Fishermen's Basin and proceeded to throw out live ducklings to be fought for by swimmers in the water. The whole town turned out to see this.

There was the fun we had buying paraffin. Cooking in *Merlin* was done on two primus stoves for which we needed both paraffin and methylated spirits. When we enquired for the former we were met with blank incomprehension and ultimately to our horror were offered '*petrole*'. We hastily explained that petrol was the last thing we wanted to put in our stoves, or we should go '*pouf*' — very graphic, this — and it was not until we found in one shop a set of instructions in French and English that we realized that '*petrole*' was the French word for paraffin. We had the same trouble with methylated spirit, of which no one had heard, but in this case a raddled old woman who came into the shop to buy a bottle of '*alcool*' put us on the right track.

And finally there was the friendliness of the inhabitants themselves, their amusement at our little knitted sailing hats, and their steadfast refusal to let us speak French. They would insist on trying out their English on us, and usually succeeded, though on one occasion my wife obstinately conducted a long conversation with a man, she speaking French and the Frenchman speaking English.

One day we decided to go a little further afield and took a bus to Wissant, a little seaside resort about half way between Calais and Boulogne. The bus was a rather decrepit single-decker with an interesting looking driver who also fulfilled the functions of conductor. The sandhills between the road and the sea were honeycombed with fortifications, and in the villages the houses on the seaward side of the road were all in ruins. A reminder of their recent history was that they were all plastered with notices in German.

After about half an hour it began to dawn on us that we were getting a very long ride for 54 francs each. This would not normally have worried us, but alas I had to confess that all our French money, apart from some small change, was in another pair of trousers in *Merlin*'s cabin! We held a hurried council of war and decided to try our luck with the driver. His reply confirmed our worst fears. It was 54 francs to go to Wissant, and it was 54 francs to go back. But the driver was most helpful; he insisted that we should not distress ourselves but should wait till we reached Wissant where he would fix everything.

When we reached Wissant the bus drew up in the village square, the main features of which were the church and the Normandy Hotel, and disgorged its passengers. The driver jumped down and engaged a young man who was standing outside the hotel in a most voluble conversation, the import of which was lost to us until the latter crossed to where we were standing and said in faultless English

'I understand you have come without any money and are worried about getting back to Calais.'

We agreed, with some surprise at finding an Englishman in such an out of the way spot, that this was so. Whereupon he told us that all we had to do was to see his father, who owned the hotel, and everything would be alright.

Still rather mystified, but considerably grateful, we went into the hotel and introduced ourselves to Monsieur Davies-Lefetz, the proprietor, who spoke French with a Welsh accent, and English with a French one. He was in fact a Welshman who had first come to Wissant in 1918 as a soldier, and after the war had married the daughter of the proprietor of the Normandy Hotel. When he took over he also took over the proprietor's name of Lefetz, tacking it on to his own.

His hospitality was instantaneous and all-embracing. He told us that he was always pleased to help English people, and that he would certainly see that we were able to pay our bus fare back to Calais. In the meantime, for as long as we cared to stay in Wissant, the Normandy Hotel was ours. Such friendliness as this, in a world where bickering and suspicion seem to be the order of the day, was almost unbelievable, and we wished that our gratitude could have taken a more tangible form than the mere thanks we were able to give him. The Normandy Hotel was clean and attractive, the meal we consumed was excellent, and the people we met were interesting. At the back of the hotel was a charming and decidedly English touch — a door bearing the simple legend — 'Gents'.

In Wissant we had one of the most fascinating experiences of our holiday. Each year on August 15th the ceremony of blessing the sea and the fishing boats is held, and when we arrived the preliminary church service was in full swing. Very soon a procession formed up and proceeded down to the seashore where several of the fishing boats had been gaily dressed with flags. The little church was soon emptied, but the hundreds of candles round the high altar and the many shrines burned steadily on, and the heavy smell of incense lingered until, several hours later, the congregation returned for a final thanksgiving prayer and a benediction.

All the village was in the procession. Headed by the priest and choir in their lace surplices, it contained all the men and women in their Sunday best, the children, many of the little girls being in their white confirmation dresses, and in the place of honour a beautifully painted statue of the Virgin Mary borne by a girl of seventeen dressed as a bride, and suitably attended. Further down the procession was a similar statue of Our Lord. The children all carried long coloured paper chains, and at intervals in the half-mile long column were priests who intoned the Litany, to which the crowd responded. Here and there among the villagers were women dressed completely in black, the widows of men lost at sea, a startlingly large number for such a small community. The whole effect was most moving in its simplicity and sincerity, and I think there were very few among the hundreds of spectators who were not affected by it as we were.

Early in the evening we reluctantly said good-bye to the Normandy Hotel and took our seats in the bus, the same vehicle that had brought us and had been patiently waiting in the square. We were interested to see that a number of seats were reserved for pregnant women or for the war-wounded, but it soon filled up and by the time we left it was a case of standing room only. We wondered idly what would happen if we met many intending passengers on the way as it was the last bus of the day. We were soon to find out.

At every stop people were waiting: at no stop was anyone left behind and soon the Babel inside the bus was incredible. But still the driver managed to cram more people in. Finally however, saturation point was reached and the seething mass round his seat and on the step came to a standstill and it appeared that he was beaten. But no! After exhausting all his powers of persuasion he gave vent to his feelings by bouncing up and down on his seat and beating on the steering wheel with his fists. Then, regaining command of himself and the situation, and crying repeatedly '*Descendez! Descendez! Descendez!* . . .' he literally forced his way off the bus, went round to the back, opened the emergency door, and proceeded to load his remaining passengers in that way. And so we ground our way into Calais. As a matter of interest we counted the number as the 27-seater emptied itself: there were 75!

Before returning to our native shores we decided to augment the children's education by letting them see a little more of the country and its capital, so we took them on a flying visit to Paris. The two days we spent there were enjoyable but hectic, and by the time we got back to Calais we were exhausted. On returning to *Merlin* however, we were quite excited to find the coupling mended and everything ready for sea. We began to feel we had been too long ashore, and were anxious to be on our way back to England. A strong sou'westerly had been blowing in the Channel for some days, and though the radio forecasts were not too good we prepared to depart the following morning. That evening on the beach at dusk, Dover Castle looked about five miles away, and as darkness fell the South Foreland Light winked out at us in the most nostalgic way.

We locked out of the inner basin at the impossible hour of 4.30 am and dropped our hook in the outer harbour. An early breakfast and preparations for leaving kept us busy, and at 9.00 am we were just on the point of getting up our anchor and proceeding to sea when we were hailed from the wharf by a young man who asked if we were going to England, and if so, did we have room for a passenger.

We held a hurried consultation, hoping for the best but prepared for the worst, for we had never carried a passenger before who was not a friend of the family, and we wondered about the additional responsibility. However, he looked a reasonable type so we motored to the wharf and picked him up. As we got sail on to *Merlin* and gathered speed down the harbour he told us his name was Colin and he was returning home after a month's hitch-hiking through France, Holland and Switzerland. He proved to be an amiable companion, popular with Anthony and Sally, and our doubts at picking him up were soon dispelled.

Outside the sou'westerly was blowing steadily and with all sail set we romped along. It was good to feel *Merlin* lifting to the waves once again, and to hear the water swooshing past her bows, and the wind in her sails. There is something in the gentle sound of a sailing boat travelling at speed that engenders great peace, and we all caught the magic of the moment as Calais was left behind and we headed for home. The day promised to be fine in spite of an ominous bank of clouds on the horizon, and overhead the sky was blue. *Merlin*'s tanned sails glowed in the morning sun and the ship was once more alive and a thing of beauty. Out in mid-Channel the sea was a deep midnight blue and we passed several large patches of seaweed. Both coasts were lost in the mist and we were alone.

About 11.00 am the wind freshened and we had to take in a reef. *Merlin* was heeled well over and her lee rail was awash, the sensation of speed being most exhilarating. Nine times out of ten reefing *Merlin*'s mainsail is a signal for the wind to drop, such is the perversity of the weather, and this is what happened to us now. Our speed decreased, we shook out the reef, but still our progress became slower and slower, and we started the engine. And then, about a mile from Dover, the wind dropped completely and left us wallowing in a fairly heavy sea. It was blisteringly hot, the tide was setting strongly to the westward, and we rolled and rolled and rolled.

For an hour we fought to cover that last mile while the sails slatted uselessly, and the gear slammed from side to side in an alarming way. Colin gradually grew quiet and couldn't finish his lunch, and it was generally rather uncomfortable. At one point the tide was so strong that we could make no progress to the east and were actually going backwards, but as we got nearer the breakwater the tide slackened and we ultimately crept in through the eastern entrance. After answering the hail from the signal bridge, and registering a mental note of thanks to Marcel and his good work on the coupling, we made for the submarine basin and were soon at anchor.

Sails were stowed and decks sluiced down and before long *Merlin* was looking as trim and ship-shape as anyone could wish. The dinghy was launched — for this time we had taken no chances but had carried it on deck — and cups of tea and cake were gratefully accepted from the mate, who could always be relied upon to produce the right thing at the right time.

It was a perfect day, and so piping all hands to bathe we climbed into the dinghy and proceeded under outboard motor round to the beach, where we spent the rest of the afternoon relaxing in the most pleasant way imaginable. In the evening we spruced ourselves up a bit and sallied ashore for dinner — our first meal on English soil for nearly a fortnight. It went down well, and when we were sitting back drinking our coffee Anthony and Sally announced that it was the best meal of the holiday. Some people have funny children!

4

A change of life

DURING the years in which we lived in Sandwich my son fell in love. In those days Thames sailing barges frequently came up the river bringing loads of timber into the town, and Anthony became fascinated with them. They would tie up at the wharf just below the bridge, and quite close to our house, and it was not long before he began to find his way aboard and got to know the skippers and crew. He was all of nine years old at the time.

There were not many of them, perhaps seven or eight barges in all, that made their occasional passage up the tortuous and shallow River Stour, each manned by two men, and very soon Anthony knew them all. He learned much about the sailing barges themselves and their unique spritsail rig, but also became frighteningly knowledgeable about the area in which they traded — broadly speaking the east and south coasts of England and the north coast of Europe — the cargoes they carried, freight rates paid, and other details of sailing barge operation. One of the most important things he learned from these homely, unassuming, but incredible sailors was about life in a small shallow draft trading vessel under sail along the sometimes treacherous coasts of these islands. For spritsail barges plied their trade in great rivers and small, and in creeks that were so shallow as to deny access to any other type of trading vessel. As one skipper proudly asserted, his barge would go wherever there had been a heavy fall of dew.

So it was no real surprise when one day Anthony announced that — with our approval — he intended to leave school as soon as he was sixteen and go to sea as the mate of a Thames barge. At the time we did not attach too much importance to this proposal, believing that all small boys go through a phase of wanting to become an engine driver, and assuming that in this instance a sailing barge was the maritime equivalent of an engine. It was not until some years later, when he was fifteen and heading for his GCE exams that we realized he was still serious. The combined efforts of ourselves, his housemaster, his headmaster, and the county vocational guidance officer failed to make any impression on him, and two days after leaving school at sixteen he was at sea as the mate of the Thames sailing barge *Portlight*. The next two and a half years neatly and efficiently changed him from a boy into a man.

Although we did not take him seriously at first, we did at least do something about it. Perhaps what we did was not the right thing, but at the time it seemed a good idea. We decided to try our hand at living on a converted sailing barge. The decision to leave Sandwich was not to be taken lightly, for we loved the place and had been there long enough to become involved in the life of the town. We lived in one of the most attractive old houses in this very historic town — the Old Customs House — which itself had a history dating back to the eleventh century, and we had not been there long before the vicar discovered we had both had some experience of amateur dramatics, and asked my wife to produce a nativity play in one of his three churches. This she did, with great success for three successive years, and arising out of this we helped to found the local dramatic society, the Barbican Players, and to establish a small theatre in an old quayside warehouse.

We were busy on the water too, and helped to start the Sandwich and District Sailing and Motor Boat Club, of which I was proud to be the first commodore. The first secretary of the club was John Court, who was roads engineer to Kent County Council, and a keen sailor. His two sons were also enthusiastic dinghy sailors. The younger, David, who was a schoolboy at the time, later became a surveyor and road engineer, and thirty years after leaving Sandwich I met him again in the Isle of Wight where he was Deputy County Surveyor. It is indeed a small world.

Once we had decided to try a floating home we began to look round for a suitable sailing barge. When war broke out in 1939 there were still several thousand barges in trade, but the war killed off most of these, and of the few that were left many were either lying derelict or were being converted into houseboats. The one we found was both.

Magnet had been converted some years previously into quite useful accommodation comprising a large square saloon, four sleeping cabins, a galley containing fitted units, a stainless steel sink and Rayburn cooker, and a bathroom with hot and cold water. The water tanks held eight tons, and the coal bunkers were equally capacious. Unfortunately, her owner, who was in the Royal Navy, had been posted abroad and had left her on her anchor in Portland harbour. She had broken adrift, gone on to the rocks, and sunk. For some time she had been left half full of water but was ultimately patched up and towed back to the Medway. She was in a sorry state when we found her. We bought her for a very reasonable figure.

Little did I realize when buying *Magnet* that I was condemning myself to two years' hard labour, for it took all of that time to pull her together. Nevertheless she provided us with a warm and comfortable home, and a life-style that was fascinating and different. To begin with we kept her at Hoo St Werburgh, a little riverside village a few miles below Rochester, where there was at that time a ramshackle and makeshift harbour, but later we moved up into the centre of Rochester itself which was much more convenient. We were literally only a few minutes from the shops and other amenities, but were moored between buoys on the river and so were completely secluded. Life on this commercial reach of the river was always novel, interesting, and at times exciting.

Our good ship *Merlin* was moored alongside *Magnet*, a very happy arrangement. The disadvantage to me personally was a two-hour journey to London each morning but at least I was able to get home every night, and once aboard *Magnet* the world could go hang. Another snag was that Anthony, for whom we had really made this move, was away at school and only home in the holidays, but Sally thrived on the river life and was a great favourite with the local watermen, one of whom told me I need never fear for her safety as there was always someone who would keep an eye on her.

One of the things that endeared Sally to these rough longshoremen was her handling of our barge boat, a 16-ft heavily-built craft propelled by sculling her over the stern with one enormous oar. Sally was only small and when she stood in the bottom of the boat could hardly see over the gunwale. To keep the blade of the oar in the water when sculling she had to hold the haft above her head and it was a comical sight to see the speed and accuracy with which she directed this large and unwieldly boat. As she came ashore one day to pick me up from the landing stage one of the watermen chuckled and said she could handle the boat as well as any of them. Heady stuff for a father's ear!

In the school holidays Anthony also entered into the life of the river with zest, and soon knew as much about what was going on as any of us. Because of his interest in boats of all types he was popular with the many men we knew who made their living on the Medway, and was a particular favourite with old George Blackman, a retired barge hand who did odd jobs and kept an eye on us. George used to come aboard every Saturday morning to check the moorings and pump out the bilge. He was a big man who had spent his whole life on the river and was full of river lore and interesting anecdotes. He was never so happy as when 'Ant'ny' was at home, and it was good to see the rapport between them. George was getting on in years, but still occasionally worked as safety boatman when

Rochester bridge was either being repaired or painted. This involved sitting in his boat downstream of the bridge and connected to it by a tremendously long warp, ready to pick up anyone who fell off. A tedious job if ever there was one, and in the winter bitterly cold, for in a small boat it was impossible to move about to keep warm. I gave George my old Home Guard greatcoat, and though it was really too small for him he said it helped to keep the cold out.

Many of the remaining working sailing barges still came into the Medway, and quite near our moorings was a barge buoy where they would tie up when waiting to unload or waiting for a cargo. Anthony was soon on familiar terms with the skippers of these barges, and particularly with one of them, 'Tubby' Blake. Tubby was an old man, and was perhaps the most fabulous character in the spritsail barge world at this time. He was well known to all and sundry, and his barge was always referred to as Tubby Blake's yacht. He sailed her singlehanded, for the very good reason that no one would sail with him on account of his dirty personal habits. He never washed, and always wore a filthy old reefer jacket, the front of which bore vivid traces of many past part-consumed meals.

But as a seaman Tubby stood supreme. He handled his engineless 80-ft 'yacht' with an ease and dexterity that was a delight to witness, and was the envy of all other sailors. Like all men of genius his art was such that what he did looked easy. He never seemed to hurry nor exert himself, always letting the wind and the tide do the work for him, and in his hands this huge boat responded like a dinghy. I well remember two examples of his seamanship at which I marvelled with envy in my heart.

The first was to see him arriving one day at the barge buoy near *Magnet*'s mooring. The anchorage was fairly crowded, with little room to manoeuvre, but Tubby came sailing up as though there were no other craft in sight. At the buoy he stopped. Just like that: he stopped, as if the barge were fitted with brakes, with the bow just touching the buoy. And the boat just stood there. She didn't drift away, or ride over the buoy, or blow off to leeward. She just stood there, waiting for her master's next move. And Tubby, with all the time in the world, waddled forward from the wheel, leaned over the bow and put a rope through the ring on the buoy and tied her up. It was sheer magic.

The other incident was even more spectacular. The four of us — and Mac, of course — were out sailing in *Merlin* one Saturday afternoon and picked up a mooring at Upnor near the *Arethusa* while we had tea. This was always a favourite spot with us for the *Arethusa* dominated this bend in the river. She belonged to the Shaftesbury Homes and was a training ship for orphan boys preparatory to their entering either the Royal or Merchant Navy. She was built in 1911 as the barque *Peking*, and along with the *Passat* and *Pamir* was one of the so-called 'Flying Ps', engaged in the Chilean nitrate trade. She was renamed *Arethusa* on becoming a training ship, and was a fine sight, and her crew of boys were very smart. On ceremonial occasions the boys manned the yards, and this was good to see.

From where we were on what amounted to a U-bend in the river we could see to our right up Chatham Reach and past the dockyard to Rochester. The other way we could see down the river and across the marshes towards Sheerness. In the distance were two sailing barges making their way upstream, assisted by a smart force 4 to 5 breeze.

The nearer of the two barges was perhaps a mile away, proceeding very steadily under topsail and was obviously going to pass us within the next fifteen minutes or so. The other barge was twice the distance away, but had all sail set, all 4,000 square feet of which was pulling hard. As soon as we saw it we all agreed that it could only be Tubby Blake coming up the river at such a fearsome speed, and so it turned out to be. He passed the other barge before he reached us, and I watched him through the binoculars as he came storming up Cockham Reach towards the corner. To my amazement there was no one on deck at the wheel. Just as he reached the bend Tubby appeared on deck, gave the wheel a twirl and rounded the corner, looked up at the sails, adjusted the main sheet, put her on course up Chatham Reach, and promptly went down below again.

It was the most astonishing display of boat handling that I had ever seen, and one I shall never forget. He told us later that he had been having his tea at the time, and seemed to think nothing of it.

Perhaps it was only natural that Anthony and Tubby should hit it off together, for they were both dedicated to sailing barges, one with so much to learn, and the other with all the practical knowledge in the world. Anthony's mother was not so sure about the friendship, but was wise enough not to forbid it, and it was not long before Anthony was sailing with Tubby in his 'yacht'. This caused us all some misgivings though we need not have worried. Anthony was only fourteen but had already shown that he was quite capable of looking after himself, and there is no doubt he learned a lot. When he came back from a trip with Tubby Blake he had to be disinfected and his clothes treated with circumspection, but the experience gained from a master seaman was invaluable, and confirmed him in his intention to leave school at the earliest opportunity and take to the sea.

Another friend that Anthony made while we were living aboard *Magnet* in the Medway was Charlie Manley. Charlie was a craftsman from the dockyard who had left to start up his own boatbuilding business. As a craftsman in wood his standards were of the highest, and any work executed by him could be guaranteed to be first class. It used to amaze

me — as a ham fisted user of wood chisels — that he could join two pieces of wood together so perfectly that you could hardly see the join. Anthony had already dabbled in boat building, and at the age of eleven had built a very serviceable dinghy, which after many years of use he had recently sold to a man who could often be seen in it on the Medway. But Charlie lifted Anthony into a different world, a world of fine tolerances and smooth finishes where the utility of the end product and its sheer beauty were of equal importance. He could not have had a better mentor, and this certainly enabled him to help when Charlie built for him *Mascotte W* a 5-ton gaff cutter, designed by John Leather on the lines of the Essex Leigh Bawley. Later, he and Sally and two friends sailed *Mascotte* to Holland.

Soon after Anthony had left school and was at sea I was approached by the BBC who wanted to do a programme on Thames sailing barges for their Monday night programme *Panorama*, which in those days was presented by Richard Dimbleby. Their plan was to sail down the Medway in a barge with Dimbleby interviewing various men who were still involved in the sailing barge world, and including Anthony as the latest recruit to the industry. They were tickled with the idea that a public school boy should adopt such an unorthodox way of life. At the time I was serving as chairman of the Kent branch of the Sailing Barge Preservation Society and was to be interviewed as such, but in the event they ran out of time and this item had to be scrubbed.

The London & Rochester Trading Co Ltd, the only local firm still owning trading barges, lent us a barge and we picked up Dimbleby and the camera crew and sailed down the river. The idea was that the interviews should be conducted as we sailed down Saltpan Reach, the last long straight stretch of the river before Sheerness, and in the dummy run before shooting started this worked perfectly. Saltpan Reach runs roughly west to east, and as the gentle breeze was due west sailing down the river was easy. But to get back to the start after the rehearsal meant tacking all the way, and this took time. On the first live run down the course we were halfway through the interviews when the cameraman suddenly discovered he had no film in his camera, so back we had to go. Fortunately the breeze had freshened a little so that tacking back to the start did not take so long.

On the next run we completed the course, though we arrived off Sheerness sooner than expected due to the freshening breeze. However, everyone seemed happy until the sound engineer had to admit that something was wrong with his equipment, and he had recorded nothing. So back we went. Dimbleby was very patient about this, indeed to my way of thinking he was far too patient. Perhaps he was used to this sort of inefficiency. However, before the next run he checked and rechecked that everything was working correctly.

This time we fairly roared down the course as the breeze was by now quite strong, and the interviewing had to be cut short. One old barge skipper who was interviewed was asked to point out Dead Mans Island as we sailed past. On the first run down he was able to do this quite readily, but on the last run we were miles past it by the time the question was put to him, and he was almost pointing at Sheerness Gasworks. The programme was a great success however when it was broadcast on the following Whit Monday, and the river scenes were beautiful.

In one way and another our life in *Magnet* was always full and varied, and though hard work was often the order of the day, we were on occasion able to drop everything, pile into *Merlin*, and slip gently down the river to the peace and quiet of the estuary. Our weekend cruising may not have been wildly adventurous but was always interesting, and to me it was the perfect antidote to a week spent in the hurly-burly of industrial London.

Our original ambition in buying the old sailing barge *Magnet* was not only to live in her but to re-rig her completely so that she would sail again. Her principal spars were not in too bad shape, but her rigging needed to be completely renewed, and her sails had actually disintegrated. It was obviously going to take time and cost money, and though we were not afraid of the hard work involved it soon became apparent that *Magnet*'s hull was very old, not to say ripe, and that even if completely re-rigged might well not be able to stand the stresses and strains involved in sailing.

Ultimately we had to abandon the idea of her ever sailing again, and be content with the fact that we had a satisfactory floating home, one that provided all we needed in the way of comfort and accommodation, and one that was the envy of many of our friends. The way of life that *Magnet* made possible was unique and presented many advantages, the principal one being that we were permanently afloat. To a family addicted to boats to a man (and a dog) this was paramount, and overrode every other consideration. Of course to begin with, when *Magnet* was moored alongside a ramshackle concrete lighter on the Hoo marshes, she only floated on the tide, and for much of the time she was surrounded by mud, but later when we moved up into Rochester, to a mooring in the centre of the town, we were afloat whatever the state of the tide, and it was glorious.

At Hoo there was quite a little community of barges, clustered round the clubroom of the Hoo Sailing Club. Living conditions were fairly primitive, but there was bags of fresh air, sky, mud, and twice a day, water. There were also several interesting people, all of whom had, like us, opted out of a conventional way of life in an attempt to get closer to nature. Amongst them were Roy 'Nobby' Clark, in his barge *William and Mary*, Arthur Bennett in *Henry*, and Dudley Pope.

Our first experience of actually sailing in a Thames barge was in *Henry*, when we took part in the Medway Barge Race one year. This was a glorious day out, and though there was not much wind we had a superb sail. *Henry*'s last commercial skipper, an old man, came down to take charge for he knew the Medway and Thames Estuary like the back of his wrinkled old hand, and I shall always remember one incident towards the end of the day which summed up for me this whole business of sailing.

We had come back into the Medway through Sheerness as the sun was setting. The wind had fallen light and we were ghosting along in silence, sitting on the coach roof and at peace with the world. Just inside the river mouth we caught up with another barge, the *Swift*, and very slowly began to pass her, only a few feet separating us. She also had her old skipper at the wheel, and as we slowly went past our skipper took his pipe out of his mouth and said quietly:

'Not so swift as she is painted!'

There was a pause, and then came back the reply

'I ain't using my motor!'

Our skipper put his pipe back in his mouth and looked straight ahead, and no other word was spoken.

Another happy memory of our days at Hoo occurred in the summer holidays, soon after we had taken over *Magnet*. Anthony had invited a schoolfriend from Sandwich to stay with us, and young Ken was so excited at the thought of a holiday in this strange world of boats, and creeks, and sailing, that he could hardly contain himself. He arrived one morning with his luggage and we installed him in one of the cabins. The only thing that marred his joy was that his mother had insisted that he continued to wear his braces, and he felt very acutely about this. We reassured him that it did not matter in the least, but he soon solved the problem himself. The memory he has left me is of him tearing down the gangplank after Anthony, who was taking him off to show him round, and as he went he threw off his braces in a grand gesture of defiance, declaiming as he went:

'This is going to be the best holiday I've ever had!'

Dudley Pope, who became a particular friend of ours, was at that time working for the *London Evening News* as their naval correspondent, but was also writing hard, and it was not long before he achieved fame as a novelist with his 'Ramage' books. He brought many interesting friends down to Hoo, including George Smith, the *Evening News* cartoonist 'Gus', who told us how long it had taken him to break through as a cartoonist, and said he could have papered his house with the rejection slips he received.

Another interesting visitor was Colin Mudie who had recently sailed the Atlantic with Patrick Ellams in the very small JOG sloop *Sopranino*. Dudley had an exactly similar boat, *Cardinal Bird*, and we helped to fit him out for a trip to the Baltic which nearly proved disastrous. The weather was bad, and his companion, a man he did not know but who came to him with the highest recommendations, was not altogether satisfactory, and poor Dudley was at one stage exhausted to the point of hallucinations, and was lucky to survive.

On a happier note Dudley and I went one night to the theatre in Bromley to see the first performance of a play written by Royce Ryton who lived with his sister Dorothy on a barge at Hoo. Dorothy was in fact the hub around which the barge community revolved. She ran the club and generally mothered the needy, including her brother who was aspiring to be a playwright. The play we went to see was being given an airing in Bromley as a preliminary to the West End, and starred a well-known retired actress who was intent on a come-back.

I don't think the play ever reached the West End, which was a pity, for it had as strong an opening as anyone could wish for, and in Act II certainly contained one of the funniest little scenes I have ever witnessed. Unfortunately Act III tailed off, became disjointed, and in fact went on and on and on until everyone lost interest. But I shall long remember the beginning of Act I, and the hilarious bit in Act II.

As the house lights went down and we were settling ourselves in our seats the curtain went up on to an empty stage and a well furnished country house type lounge. Before we had time to take it all in however we were jolted out of our seats by a very loud revolver shot off-stage, and a young and pretty girl came staggering on and collapsed in a heap. She was followed by an older woman with a smoking revolver in her hand and a murderous expression on her face, who viciously pumped three more shots into the recumbent body. The effect was dramatic in the extreme.

They were, of course, only rehearsing a scene from a play, and after that opening it settled down to become a fairly straightforward, well written, comedy, dealing with all the problems of casting, etc, associated with producing a play. Act II took place that same afternoon when they were rehearsing another scene from the play. They were short of one or two characters in this scene, and then the vicar happened to call and was impressed into service. They stood the poor man up in the centre of the stage, gave him a script, and as they prowled round him the scene became hilarious. Who the actor was who played the vicar I don't know, but his facial expressions at some of the lines he had to utter were exquisite. Though this particular play may not have reached the West End, Royce Ryton did ultimately hit the big time, and deservedly so.

Life in the little barge settlement at Hoo was always interesting, and even when there were no events of major importance to report, the interplay between members of this small community frequently turned up something amusing. No doubt these were often exaggerated, as was the suspected romance between two very mature and sober residents. Rumours began to fly but there was absolutely no evidence. They were never seen alone together, and many were inclined to dismiss the whole thing as gossip. And then one night there was a heavy fall of snow. In the morning the site was covered in a pristine mantle of white — except for one tell-tale set of male footprints, leading from the lady's door to that of her boyfriend.

One advantage of this little barge harbour at Hoo where your boat took the ground each tide was that you normally did not need to pump out the bilges. Every barge was fitted with a large wooden plug at its after end, and all that was necessary when bilge water had collected was to knock out this plug after the tide had left her, and let gravity do the rest. It was of course important to remember to replace the plug before the tide returned, otherwise the barge would fill, and although the hole was relatively small, once there was a foot or two of water outside, the pressure forcing water in was very great, and getting the plug back in became more difficult and a very wetting operation.

Occasionally we had a few anxious moments through forgetfulness, but a neighbour of ours nearly did sink his barge completely. He worked in the City and went off one morning as usual, forgetting that the plug was out and that the tide was already on the make. It must have been an hour or two before he remembered, for it was at least 10 o'clock before he returned, in a considerable state of mind, not at all the neat and tidy city gent who had left earlier in his black coat and striped trousers, with bowler hat, tightly rolled umbrella and briefcase, but a very hot and flustered individual with his bowler hat over his eyes, clutching his umbrella and briefcase as if they were sword and buckler, and with the most worried expression I ever saw on any man's face. His home was already half full of water, but luckily he was able to locate the bung and replace it, and after many hours back-breaking work on the bilge pump managed to transfer the water back to the outside of the boat where it rightly belonged.

I have often wondered what his thoughts were on the train coming back to Hoo, he must have suffered agonies every time it slowed down or stopped, knowing that every second the water was pouring in through that hole in the bottom. I don't think he would forget again.

The great snag about living at Hoo was the daily journey to town, and many of my colleagues at work thought I was mad. Perhaps I was. I left home at 6.00 am and rode my bicycle, come rain or shine, for about a mile across the marshes to the little village of Hoo St Werbergh. Here a friendly sub-postmaster let me leave it at the back of his shop and I caught the first bus into Rochester, via Strood. At Strood station I left the bus in time to catch the 7.15 train to Waterloo. This train had already called at Gillingham, Chatham and Rochester, and was packed with a crowd of sullen, morose and grumpy people who were not really happy at having had to get up so early. I travelled on this train, in the same compartment of the same coach, with the same people, almost every day of my working life, for over seven years, and in all that time only got to know three people. A few others did return my 'good morning' on occasion, but the majority preserved an impenetrable silence.

In about an hour's time the train decanted some of us on to the platform at Waterloo Junction Station, and after a brisk walk across the road to the main line station I caught another train to Clapham Junction. Here I had the choice of either walking or waiting for a bus to take me down to Battersea Bridge, where I eventually arrived at my place of work, feeling as well as could be expected. At night the process was reversed, took a little longer, and was more tiring.

When we moved *Magnet* up into Rochester we were a little closer to civilization, but because we were moored out in the river there was very little saving of time for me in the mornings. The only communication with the shore was by dinghy, there being a very efficient landing pontoon about 150 yards downstream at Ship Pier, and another one a little further away in the other direction at Blue Boar Pier. The mooring was directly opposite a derelict wharf where it was possible to land at, or near, high tide, and where it was also possible for friends to come and hail us, though my recollection of this latter facility is that it was more of a nuisance than anything else. But apart from this tenuous link we were isolated, gloriously and completely cut off from the world, and yet within five minutes we could be in the centre of Rochester High Street, with all its shops and facilities.

The snag of course was that everything that was needed to sustain life aboard, even such basic items as bread and milk, had to be humped. There were no deliveries whatsoever. The postman never called, and we had to collect our mail from Rochester Post Office. How many pints of milk we drank per day I can't remember, but each and every one had to be carried about half a mile from the dairy at the bottom of Star Hill, loaded into the dinghy, and then off-loaded on to *Magnet*'s deck.

Drinking water, which could have been a serious problem, turned out to be no problem at all, for the Medway Conservancy Authorities maintained a water barge for the convenience of visiting ships, and whenever we wanted water they would come alongside and fill us up. *Magnet* had capacious tanks and I used to buy eight tons at a time — at some ridiculous figure such as 2/6d per ton. The water barge men became firm friends and were frequent callers for we had a very efficient bathroom and used a lot of water. In fact, they often said they were amazed at the amount we got through, and could not imagine what we did with it.

Coal was a bit of a problem, mainly because it had to be carried from the town, and it was heavy and dirty. We had two coal burning stoves, a Rayburn cooker in the galley and a Courtier stove in the saloon, and these two devices between them were as good as any central heating system. The Rayburn of course provided us with an ample supply of piping hot water, and the galley, which had fitted units and a stainless steel sink, was always warm. The barge was also light and airy for there were many skylights and a row of port holes on each side of the coach roof, conveniently placed at eye level, so that you could see what was going on outside in the river.

All the ventilation was naturally overhead, as the boat itself was surrounded by water, and the extraordinary thing was that skylights could always be kept open, except perhaps in the heaviest of rain, and ventilation was always good, but there were never any draughts. The main hatch was usually kept open, and even in the bitterest weather the heat did not escape. After working on deck in a freezing wind it was a joy to come down the main companionway, for this was like sinking into a hot bath.

But back to the problem of coal supplies. The owner of the derelict wharf allowed me to keep a stock of coal there, but alas it had to be sacked and transported across in the dinghy at high tide, and there were times when this became a bit of a chore. There was also the occasion when, at an exceptionally high spring tide, the wharf was flooded to a depth of a foot or more and I lost a ton of coke which floated away downstream on the ebb.

We had other friends besides the water barge men, and these were the lightermen who were continually bringing up lighters full of coal to Rochester gas works. Occasionally they would leave a lighter alongside overnight, a practice to which we had no objection for they were always friendly and polite, and one day one of them said that he hoped we were taking advantage of this and filling our coal bunkers from the lighter. This suggestion startled me somewhat, for the thought of using gas works coal had not occurred to me, but he seemed rather hurt that we were not helping ourselves, and asked me why I thought they were leaving the lighters alongside. The next time they came he and his mates filled our bunkers themselves, which was a very kind gesture, but one we had to discourage. Apart from the ethics of the situation the coal was of very poor quality for household use, and burned with a thick yellowy-green smoke that could be seen for miles!

The reach of the River Medway we were moored in was known as Limehouse Reach, a romantic sounding name but one without the Chinatown connection of its London River counterpart. But it was an interesting reach and represented the limit of navigation for the largest ships that visited the port of Rochester, up to about 10,000 tons. It ran roughly north and south, on the west side being the town, but the east side was open marshland. At the northern end, where the river did a U-bend into Bridge Reach, lay Strood, where there was much commercial activity, including a cement works whose tall chimney wore a perpetual plume of white smoke, night and day. To leeward of the cement works the ground was as white as if it had been snowing.

The big foreign ships that came to the moorings in Limehouse Reach were of many nationalities, though predominantly Scandinavian, German, or Dutch. Many of them came regularly, and became quite familiar to us, and there was always activity and interest, literally within a few yards of our own mooring. There were fairly frequent attempts by the crews of visiting ships to sell us duty-free cigarettes and liquor, and it was commonplace to be stopped and questioned by Customs men on going ashore. Our biggest excitement happened late one night when the crew of a German ship mutinied and attacked the officers with knives. The latter barricaded themselves on the bridge and blew a series of SOS signals on the whistle. The harbour police soon arrived, and the affair fizzled out, so that apart from our sleep being disturbed we had no trouble.

The police launch never seemed to be very far away and was a great comfort as it did regular patrols. One day it arrived alongside *Magnet* and on its deck was a small antique occasional table, as incongruous a sight as if the skipper had been carrying an umbrella. They asked if the table was ours, and explained that there had been a robbery at Pickford's warehouse in Canterbury where all our furniture was stored, and this was one of the items they had managed to recover.

If we had to leave the dinghy unattended at Ship Pier it was very necessary to lock the oars to the boat, otherwise there was a risk that someone would borrow it and forget to return it. This did not often happen but could be very irritating when it did. The rowlocks we normally carried with us, but the oars were secured cunningly by a length of chain and a padlock, to which we all had a key.

There was another risk connected with the unattended dinghy, and this concerned its drain plug. This was a screwed brass fitting in the bottom of the boat, and on one occasion someone managed to unscrew it while we were away, whereupon of course the dinghy filled with water. We had been taking part in a Drama Festival in London and arrived home at 1.30 am so were not pleased to find we could not use the dinghy. Fortunately the humourist who had removed the plug had left it in the boat, so that all we had to do was replace it and bale out the water.

Amateur dramatics began to play a bigger and bigger part in our lives, and our home life suffered accordingly. For several years I was secretary of the Medway Theatre Guild, an organization of 26 amateur dramatic societies in the Medway Towns, and apart from the administrative work this kept me busy producing, acting, and stage-managing for various groups. My wife became well known locally as an actress and producer, and achieved considerable success in various drama festivals. Perhaps the climax of her work was to produce a One Act Play called *Night* for a local society, for this not only did well in the Kent County One Act Play Festival (it shared second place with a play I had produced for another society) but it went on to beat all-comers in England, and we had the honour of representing England in the national final of the competition in London. We were runners-up in this final to Scotland, though Wendy Hiller, one of the adjudicators, told us afterwards she thought we ought to have won. However our disappointment was mitigated by the fun of giving two performances in the West End, at the old Scala theatre in Charlotte Street.

Each summer the Medway Theatre Guild put on a full length open air Shakespeare play in Gillingham Park for Gillingham corporation — these being the days before television had swamped our homes with second-rate American serials and other rubbish. We prided ourselves on the professional standard we achieved, and indeed several of our actors went on to make their career in the theatre. One year we did *A Midsummer Night's Dream*, which my wife produced, and in which one of the lovers was played by a young actor Peter Palmer, while another Peter — Peter Jackson — played Oberon. Both these Peters went on to become

Royal Shakespeare Company players.

'The Dream' was a busy and happy production for me, for as well as being stage manager I also played Peter Quince, a gem of a character part. Two incidents still bring a smile to my face. We played in front of a shrubbery in the park, with several natural entrances and exits, and in one scene Peter Palmer, playing Lysander, (or was it Demetrius?) had to make an exit and then re-enter a few minutes later. As it was not worth going all the way back to the dressing rooms he lay down under a bush to wait for his cue, and while he was there I had to make an entrance from the same spot and so went past him. Now, we had imported a number of young girls from a local school to act as fairies, and some of these had taken a shine to Peter, who was tall, dark and handsome. When I passed him lying there in the shrubbery he was being pestered by three of these not so bashful young maidens, one of whom was crawling all over him saying 'Go on, give us a kiss!' To his credit he was trying desperately to get rid of her, and was whispering urgently 'Go away! Go away!' but was having little success. The whole thing was quite innocent but I pretended to be shocked and reproved him. Afterwards I never let him forget it, always greeting him as 'that great romantic actor!'

The other memory concerned Peter Jackson who was tall and willowy, and for whom as Oberon we had provided a very smart wig with an upswept hair-do. The Gillingham Park authorities had asked whether we wanted the park closed to the public during our dress rehearsal, but thinking it might be good for publicity I suggested they kept it open. This was a great mistake for we attracted a mob of unruly kids who had something less than a reverent attitude to what we were doing. When they first caught sight of Peter in his Oberon wig a great cry went up 'Yah! Cocoanut bonce!' and poor Peter had to be soothed before he would proceed.

The following year we put on *Twelfth Night*, which I produced, with my wife playing Viola. Peter Jackson played Sir Andrew Aguecheek, and his great friend Ken Post, who was as short and rotund as Peter was tall and slim, played opposite him as Sir Toby Belch. They were splendid together and a great success, and Ken needed no padding for the part of Sir Toby. Many photographs were taken during the dress rehearsal and Ken came down to *Magnet* one evening to see the proofs.

As the tide was right I told him to come to the wharf and give us a hail, and I would then come over in the dinghy and pick him up. All went well until he clambered down the few feet from the top of the wharf, looking very large for such a small boat. He put one foot in the dinghy but refused to let go of the wharf, and I found it quite impossible to hold the boat against the enormous pressure tending to push it away from the wharf. Gradually the gap widened and ultimately something had to give, and Ken let go. With one gigantic splash, the like of which I had never seen, he fell in between the boat and the wharf and disappeared from view — all 22 stone of him.

I suppose it was inevitable, but if he had only told me he was quite unused to boats and had never been in a dinghy in his life I would have thought several times before inviting him out to *Magnet*. For a moment or two he really thought he was going to drown, but the water was not more than four feet deep so there was relatively little danger. The problem was how to get him into the dinghy for he was very wet and very frightened.

It was a considerable struggle, and by the time he was in I was as wet as he was and the dinghy was half full of water. The funny side of it then hit me and I started to laugh, and even Ken had to admit that the situation contained the elements of humour. Getting him aboard the barge was tricky and I finally hoisted him up with a block and tackle! We put him in the bathroom with towels but I had no clothes that would go anywhere near him. Fortunately, Pat was aboard at the time, typing, and she volunteered to go to Ken's home and bring dry clothes, which she did. In the meantime he sat swathed in blankets — and looked at the *Twelfth Night* photographs.

Later when he went ashore I took him to Ship Pier, the nearest pontoon landing place, and having lashed the dinghy securely to the pontoon managed to roll him on to it. His relief on finding himself once more on terra firma was beautiful to behold, and he said fervently:

'I shall never go in a boat again as long as I live!'

I smiled and replied with equal fervour:

'Not in one of mine you won't!'

5

A weekend cruise

ALL was bustle aboard the sailing barge *Magnet* on Friday afternoon as we prepared for a short weekend cruise in *Merlin*. There should really have been no bustle at all, for we were quite used to casting off from our floating home for short periods, but there always seem to be so many things to do at the last minute. Though we planned to leave at the top of the tide, so as to carry the ebb all the way down the Medway from Rochester, we were invariably late and leaving in a hurry.

While I was checking to see that we had enough water aboard, and paraffin both for cooking and lighting, my wife was fussing over the food and clothing we were going to take. At the same time she was keeping an eye on the children who were trying to make up their minds what to take to read and to amuse themselves with if they got bored. The children were responsible for their own clothes but there was a need to supervise them and to ensure they packed warm sweaters. It can get very cold on a boat, particularly in the evenings, and it is a good rule always to take one sweater more than you think you will need. The only member of the crew who was not making last minute preparations was Mac, who had long since sensed the excitement in the air and was already sitting in *Merlin*'s cockpit, wondering why on earth these humans took so long to get ready.

Though there was plenty of commercial activity in Limehouse Reach our mooring was not noisy, and when going aboard, the feeling of seclusion and severance from the more hectic life ashore began as soon as you left the landing stage in the dinghy. Once on board you were cut off from the city traffic with its noise and fumes, there were no crowds to jostle you, and no telephones. You were indeed entering another world. An additional bonus was to be able to sail away down the river in *Merlin* and leave the sophistication of the city completely behind. On this Friday afternoon Mac was not the only one who was looking forward to getting away.

At last the preparations for departure were complete, stores were all aboard *Merlin*, and we were able to climb down from *Magnet*'s deck. At the last minute we were hailed from the wharf by two young friends of the children who wanted to come aboard. This was rather awkward as we were already late, but after a hurried consultation Anthony rowed over in the dinghy to invite them to come with us a few miles down to Gillingham, where we could put them ashore. They accepted this invitation with glee and were soon back aboard, full of excitement at the prospect of a sail.

Merlin was lying with her head up-tide and was facing almost due north. What breeze there was was westerly, tending to pin her against the side of *Magnet*, but we were blanketed by the high ground on which Rochester was built, and the breeze was very fluky. The ebb had been running for several hours but in the sheltered position where we lay was not strong. Getting away was comparatively simple. The jib and main were both set, but not sheeted in, and the children on the foredeck unhitched the for'ard mooring warp from her sansom post and threw it on the barge's deck where we could pick it up again when we returned. Then with the boathook Anthony pushed *Merlin*'s head off into the stream. Very slowly the tide took her and when she was head to wind the jib was sheeted in aback and her head began to come round with more speed. The stern warp was then cast off in the same way, and we were off. Gradually, *Merlin* gathered way and came under control, and very soon we were at the bend of the river and turning into the two-mile stretch of Chatham Reach. As we cleared the town the breeze became steadier, and though it was only blowing force 2-3 *Merlin* began to slip along very satisfactorily.

Chatham Reach lies almost due north-east, so we had a beam wind and no problems. On our right as we sailed gently past were the wharves and buildings of the dockyard, with behind them on the hill the little church of St Mary. On the left was flat, open country to the high ground of Frindsbury about two miles away, and very soon we passed the entrance to Whitewall Creek, a muddy inlet where several old barges were spending the rest of their days.

Further down this reach of the river on the port hand lie the twin villages of Upper and Lower Upnor, and the ill fated Upnor Castle. The castle was originally built in 1560 when a Spanish invasion was threatening, but when the Armada failed in 1588, and a lasting peace was believed to have been established, it ceased to have much importance. In 1667, after several years of war with the Dutch and the French, a Dutch fleet under de Ruyter sailed up the Thames and the Medway and found us woefully equipped to deal with them. Upnor Castle proved to be almost useless, and after the Peace of Breda was signed in the same year it was

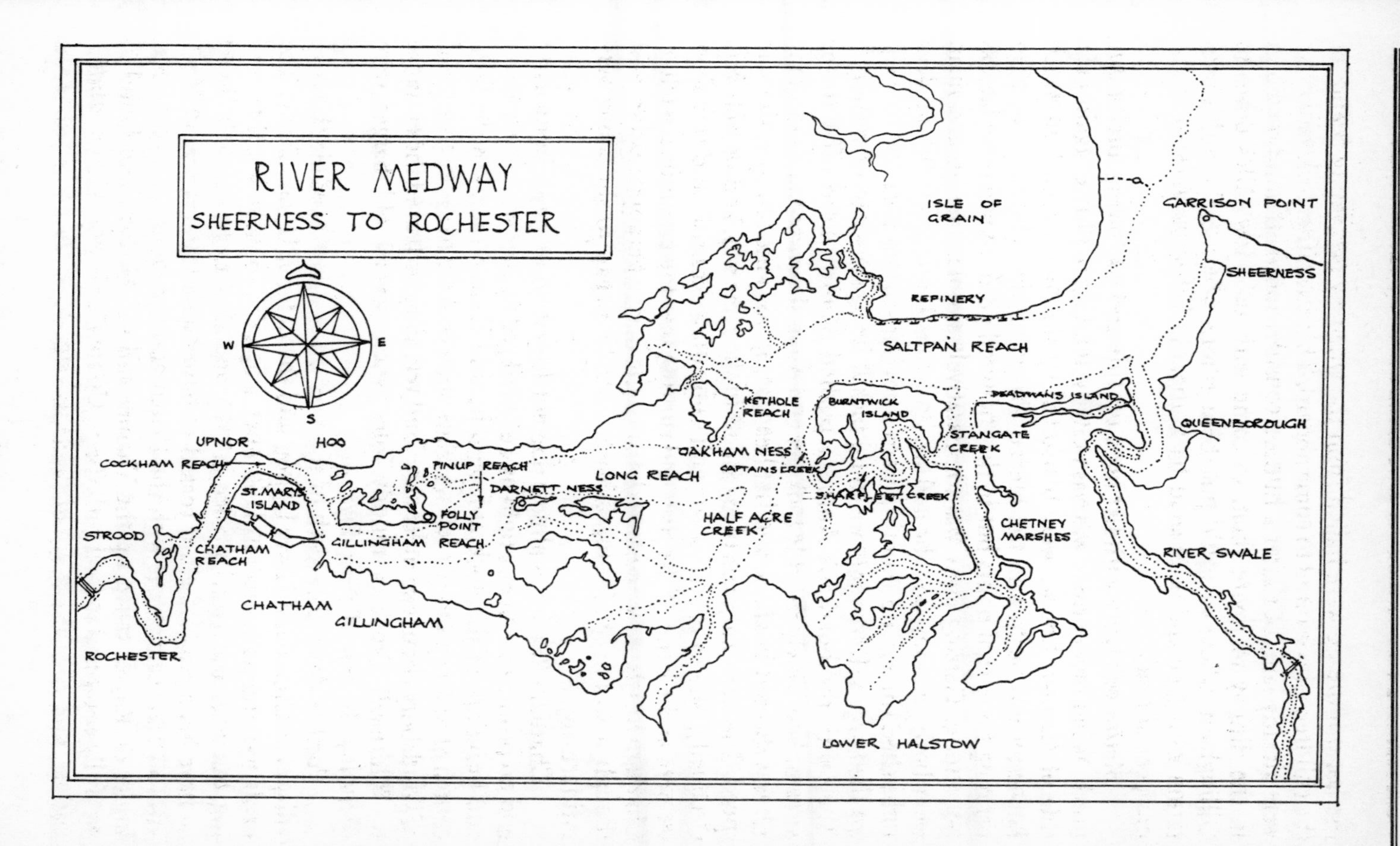
RIVER MEDWAY
SHEERNESS TO ROCHESTER
W
E
S
ISLE OF GRAIN
GARRISON POINT
SHEERNESS
REFINERY
SALTPAN REACH
DEADMANS ISLAND
QUEENBOROUGH
KETHOLE REACH
BURNTWICK ISLAND
STANGATE CREEK
UPNOR
HOO
OAKHAM NESS
COCKHAM REACH
PINUP REACH
LONG REACH
CAPTAINS CREEK
DARNETT NESS
SHARFLEET CREEK
ST. MARYS ISLAND
FOLLY POINT
HALF ACRE CREEK
CHETNEY MARSHES
STROOD
CHATHAM REACH
GILLINGHAM REACH
RIVER SWALE
CHATHAM
GILLINGHAM
ROCHESTER
LOWER HALSTOW

only ever used as an ammunition store.

At Lower Upnor the river does a tremendous U-bend to the right, and in the bight of the bend is, or was, moored the Training Ship *Arethusa* (ex-*Peking*) fully rigged and looking very smart. With Cockham Woods as a background this is one of the prettiest corners on the whole river, and one where the nightingales still sing in the spring.

As we rounded the bend the grown-ups retired below to prepare tea, leaving the children in charge. Anthony and Sally were both now quite capable of handling *Merlin* and enjoyed the responsibility of being left on their own. Being older Anthony had had more experience and had also done a trip or two as extra mate in a sailing barge, so he knew what he was about. Perhaps this is where he had acquired the diverting habit of delivering his orders in a stentorian voice more suited to a fully-rigged ship than a 7-ton cutter, and incidentally in language so lucid as to leave the crew in little doubt as to his opinion of either their capabilities or their antecedents. Gliding quietly down Gillingham Reach we were treated to a vocal display from the temporary skipper which reduced us to hysterics, and raised strange echoes from several anchored men-of-war.

Off Gillingham Strand, where we anchored for tea, our young friends had, reluctantly, to leave us and I put them ashore in the dinghy. The sun was already getting low and the breeze was dying with it, so that while I was away my wife and the children set sail and got the anchor up. As I pulled back towards *Merlin* she presented a wonderful sight. Her white hull glistened and shone in the warm evening light, and her tanned sails, all identically curved in the light westerly breeze, stood out against the low distant line of the marsh. Truly a sight to gladden an owner's heart.

The next two hours were idyllic. The breeze fell light but was enough to keep the sails filled, and with the last of the ebb under her *Merlin* sailed serenely down the river, taking us steadily and quietly on our way. The sun sank lower and lower and we were treated to one of those spectacular sunsets when the western sky is full of impossible shades of red, and overhead the colour gradually deepens until it is almost a midnight blue. We all fell silent under the magic of the moment, while astern of us the water, gently rippling by our movement through it, reflected the sunset, and ahead showed us all the colours of mother of pearl.

We had decided to spend the night in Stangate Creek, and as we turned to glide in, the light had almost gone. Automatically speaking in whispers so as not to destroy the peace of the evening we agreed to sail up the creek as far as the breeze, which was now rapidly failing, would take us. In fact the breeze held, and with the young flood under us, we

Sandwich Quay, several tortuous miles from the sea. Now thronged with small boats, but in Merlin's *day deserted, apart from the occasional sailing barge.*

Overlooking Sandwich, the great Roman Fort of Rutupiae (Richborough).

Our first adventure was to Harty Ferry on the River Swale, where we anchored off the Ferry Inn.

Mascotte W, *the 5-ton cutter that Charlie Manley and Anthony built.* Mascotte *was later sailed to Belgium and Holland by Anthony, Sally, Pat, and friends.*

The Thames Sailing Barge Lord Roberts *that Anthony and I bought and converted for charter work. She is shown here at Lower Halstow, an old Kentish creekside village where Sir Francis Drake learned to sail as a boy.*

The Saxon Church at Lower Halstow.

Peradventure was so well balanced that in this sort of a breeze (Force 4) she would sail herself.

Our idyllic mooring in the Beaulieu River above Bucklers Hard. The boat on the next mooring ahead is Ardglass, *another Harrison Butler 7-tonner.*

Above Peradventure *becalmed in the Solent. Time to study her beautiful lines.*

Below Peradventure*'s bowsprit pointing over the sparkling water.*

Below *Moored in Yarmouth harbour. Time to study the other boats.*

Above *Cockpit and boom gallows, which we had fitted to give us standing headroom.*
Below Peradventure *on starboard tack.*

Below *Off Beaulieu River entrance. Gurnard and the Isle of Wight to port.*

Left *A peaceful anchorage in the Western Haven, Newtown River.*

Below left *Sunset in Newtown.*

Right Narija *in Stangate Creek, River Medway.*

Far right Narija*'s wheelhouse, the helmsman's view.*

Right *Down below looking forward into the wheelhouse.*

Far right *From* Narija*'s well-equipped galley, looking aft.*

Early morning peace in Stangate Creek.

Another peaceful spot, the landing pontoon at Folly Pier, Medina River, Isle of Wight.

The end of a perfect sail — bringing the dinghy ashore.

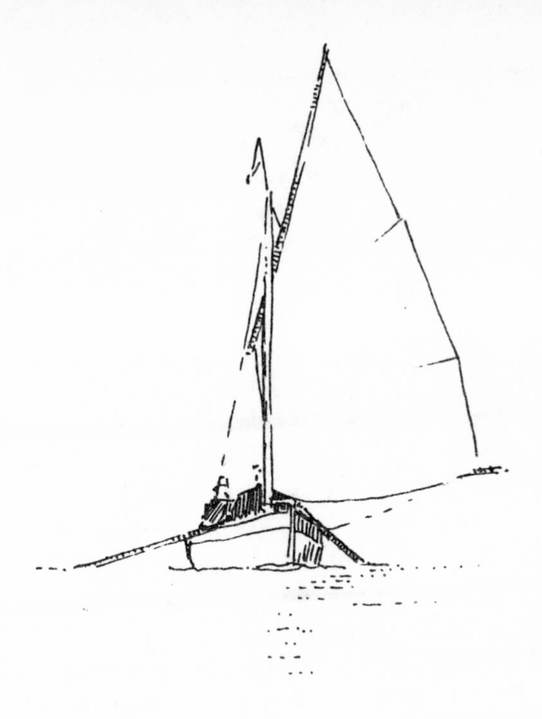

were able to reach Slaughterhouse Point where the creek divides, and turning to starboard we brought up quietly in about two fathoms of water. It was not long before sails were stowed, ropes coiled, and the riding light lit and hoisted up the forestay.

Before turning in we stood in the cockpit for a moment listening to the silence. The only sounds were the occasional rustling of the tide against the hull as the flood slowly strengthened. To our north we could see the twinkling lights of the oil refinery on the Isle of Grain, and westwards the loom of the Medway Towns' lights. The breeze died completely and *Merlin* and her crew were at peace.

In the morning the children were up early and rigged the dinghy for a sail. They tried desperately hard to be quiet so as not to wake us, but down below sounds are magnified, and though they spoke in stage whispers, the noise they made, Mac's excited scampering around, and Sally's occasional giggling, inevitably woke us and we had to smile. Once they had cast-off peace returned but sleep was now impossible and there was nothing for it but to get up. Another day had begun.

On deck there had been a heavy dew and the creek was covered in a fine mist, through which the sun was beginning to show. It promised to be another warm and sunny day, though perhaps more suited to sunbathing than to sailing. As I took down the riding light and blew it out I could see the dinghy in the distance. There was not a lot of wind but they were managing to get along, and they must have seen the activity on *Merlin*'s deck for they soon headed towards her, sensing that breakfast was on the way. Sally was at the helm and she came alongside in masterly fashion without, as they say, breaking an egg.

Over breakfast we discussed plans for the day. Unless the breeze was very much stronger than yesterday we were not going to get very far, but we all looked forward to a day of gentle sailing, with the general object of bringing up for the night at Harty Ferry in the River Swale. I personally had a desire to explore Sharfleet Creek on the way out of Stangate, and felt that as we would be on a rising tide we might even be able to circumnavigate Burntwick Island and come out into the Medway through Captain's Creek. After consulting the chart and discussing likely depths of water in the shallow parts the family decided to humour me, and agreed that it might even be a bit of an adventure.

The flood was making quite strongly by the time we were ready to go, and I was quite sure there would be enough water over the mud flats between Sharfleet and Captain's Creek when we got there. My main worry was that once we were out into the Medway we would have the full strength of a spring tide against us and progress might be slow. High water was at 13.45 by which time we needed to be well into the Swale in order to have enough water through the shallows off Fowley Island. The breeze was sou'westerly, about force 3, and provided it did not die on us this was ideal.

The anchor came up smartly at 10.45 and we were on our way. The anchor had brought up quite a lot of Medway mud, but with buckets of sea water and a stiff broom this was soon cleared and the decks sluiced down. This simple operation was always very satisfying, and with my wife on the helm the children and I enjoyed our little 'paddle' as we proceeded slowly down Stangate against the flood tide.

At the entrance to Sharfleet we turned sharply to port and for a few moments it looked as though we were going to be headed by the wind, but by hugging the mud flats on the port hand we managed to avoid tacking, and soon picked up speed as we sailed up the first reach. At the end of this reach is a U-bend which took us through the wind, but here there was plenty of water and navigation was easy. *Merlin* went creaming down this stretch of the Creek, which is perhaps half a mile long, but then the channel bends once more sharply to starboard.

The next mile was the tricky bit, and where, if we were not careful, we would go on the mud. The flats were now covered and we were surrounded by a large expanse of water with only a few low lying islands to show us where the land lay. But appearances are very deceptive for the water is very shallow and the channel narrow. Its general direction however is westerly and at each end there is a beacon. If you can sail between these two you will not go far wrong, but unfortunately with the wind in the sou'west it was difficult to keep in the best water. With Anthony and Sally on the lead however, shouting out the depths, we were able to keep roughly in the channel where there was up to two fathoms of water. This shoaled rapidly to a very few feet at each side, and there were several anxious moments as we hurriedly changed course. The beacon we were aiming for had a triangular topmark and marked the beginning of Captain's Creek, and as we drew nearer to it the water gradually deepened and we were able to relax. On our port hand the nearest solid land was a mile or more away, and ahead was the Medway where we could already see the buoys marking the big ship channel.

As we skirted Burntwick Island on our starboard hand and rounded Sharp Ness we met the full force of the tide, but the breeze was steady and we fairly romped through the water, though our progress over the ground was necessarily much slower. Down Saltpan Reach we sailed for about two and a half miles until we reached the buoy marking the entrance to the River Swale. Here we turned sharply to starboard and could see Queenborough ahead of us.

We have a love-hate relationship with Queenborough. We love its history, its connection with Edward III and his Queen Philippa, and later with Lord Nelson and Lady Hamilton, but we hate the modern day industry which has despoiled the town, and particularly the glue works. The town's history stretches way back to before the Norman Conquest when there was a Saxon fort here, but it was Edward III who gave it its name. In 1361 he built a large castle, and made the town a free borough in honour of his Queen. We had a particular interest in this royal lady since the house in Sandwich where we had lived, the Old Customs House, was reputed to have housed Queen Philippa while she was waiting for a fair wind to take her to Calais to join her husband in 1347. The principal bedroom in the house was known as Queen Philippa's room.

The castle became the official residence of the Lord Warden of the Cinque Ports in 1582, and had the honour of entertaining Queen Elizabeth I. Sir Francis Drake also visited the place, but then he knew the area well for when he was a boy his father had been vicar of nearby Upchurch. Much later in its history Lord Nelson stayed in Queenborough, as did Lady Hamilton. So it can be said that the town has had a romantic

Queenborough

history, but alas! today the glue works, with its overpowering stench, dominates all, and when the wind is south-easterly the moorings become quite untenable. We were in the habit of visiting Queenborough frequently when the wind was not in this quarter, and found it delightful. There was good shelter on the moorings and a splendidly clean landing hard, at the head of which was (and still is) 'The Old House at Home', as pleasant a waterfront pub as one could wish.

But today we passed by. Tide time was not far off and we knew there might be a delay at Kingsferry Bridge which was another two miles further on. The bridge is the only link between the Isle of Sheppey and the mainland, and carries both road and railway running from Sittingbourne to Sheerness. It has a lifting span, and subject to railway traffic will always be opened on request for vessels with fixed masts. There are two ways of requesting permission to pass through, one being to hoist a bucket or similar large object up into the rigging and then wait until the bridge opens, always assuming that the bridge keeper has seen your signal and is proposing to do something about it. The other method, which is better and was much preferred by the children, is to go ashore and contact the bridge keeper in person, for he will then tell you what the delay is likely to be, and at least you will then know where you are.

On this occasion we arrived at the bridge at 13.50, almost exactly on the top of the tide, and within a few minutes were ashore, Mac, as usual, leading the way. Up in the control room the bridge keeper told us that as soon as the 2 o'clock from Sittingbourne had gone through he would open for us, and this was good news indeed as it meant a wait of only about twenty minutes. Sure enough at about 14.20 the Sittingbourne train came clanking over the bridge, and soon after that the lifting span began slowly to rise. We were all ready, and with the benefit of a beam wind were on our way slowly through the opening.

We had delayed eating our sandwiches until we were through the bridge, and by this time were all famished, so we now tucked into them as we sailed serenely down the river towards Harty, about seven miles away. Dessert consisted of apples and bananas, after which the kettle was put on and steaming mugs of coffee were served in the cockpit. The breeze held good and we made gentle but satisfactory progress.

Half a mile from Kingsferry we passed on the starboard hand Ridham Dock, a commercial wharf serving a large paper works, and another half mile or so from this came to the old Elmley Ferry where, it is claimed, James II embarked in a hoy in an attempt to flee the country in 1688. Later he succeeded in getting away from Faversham, a few miles to the east, and he must have been relieved when his flight was all over, for no more desolate and lonely place than these marshes can be imagined for a king who was abandoning his kingdom.

As we had been making good time we found more water between Elmley Ferry and Fowley Island than we had expected, and had no problems in this last very pleasant run down to Harty Ferry, which had long been a favourite anchorage of ours. There were several boats already here, this being a popular Saturday night rendezvous, but we had no difficulty in finding a suitable place to anchor almost opposite the Ferry House Inn.

That evening after a leisurely meal we went ashore to the inn and sat outside in the evening sunshine looking down on the anchorage. There were several other sailing families there, one of whom we already knew, and the time passed all too quickly as we renewed old friendships and made new ones.

Sunday morning dawned bright and clear with no trace of the mist which was present the day before, and there was a high layer of alto-cirrus cloud that suggested the possibility of an end to the fine spell we had been enjoying. The breeze was still sou'westerly and was certainly a shade stronger than yeasterday, and I had a feeling that it might pipe up a bit during the day.

Our plan was to return to the Medway by completing the circumnavigation of Sheppey, and with high water scheduled for 15.15 hours this meant a reasonably early start in order to make full use of the flood up the river. A shore party was consequently despatched immediately after breakfast with the dual purpose of giving Mac another run (he had already been ashore once), and also to fill our water containers from the spring near the hard, this being in our opinion the finest drinking water in the whole of the Medway area.

We were off at 08.30 and with a smart following breeze were soon making good progress. As we passed the Horse Sand just below Harty I

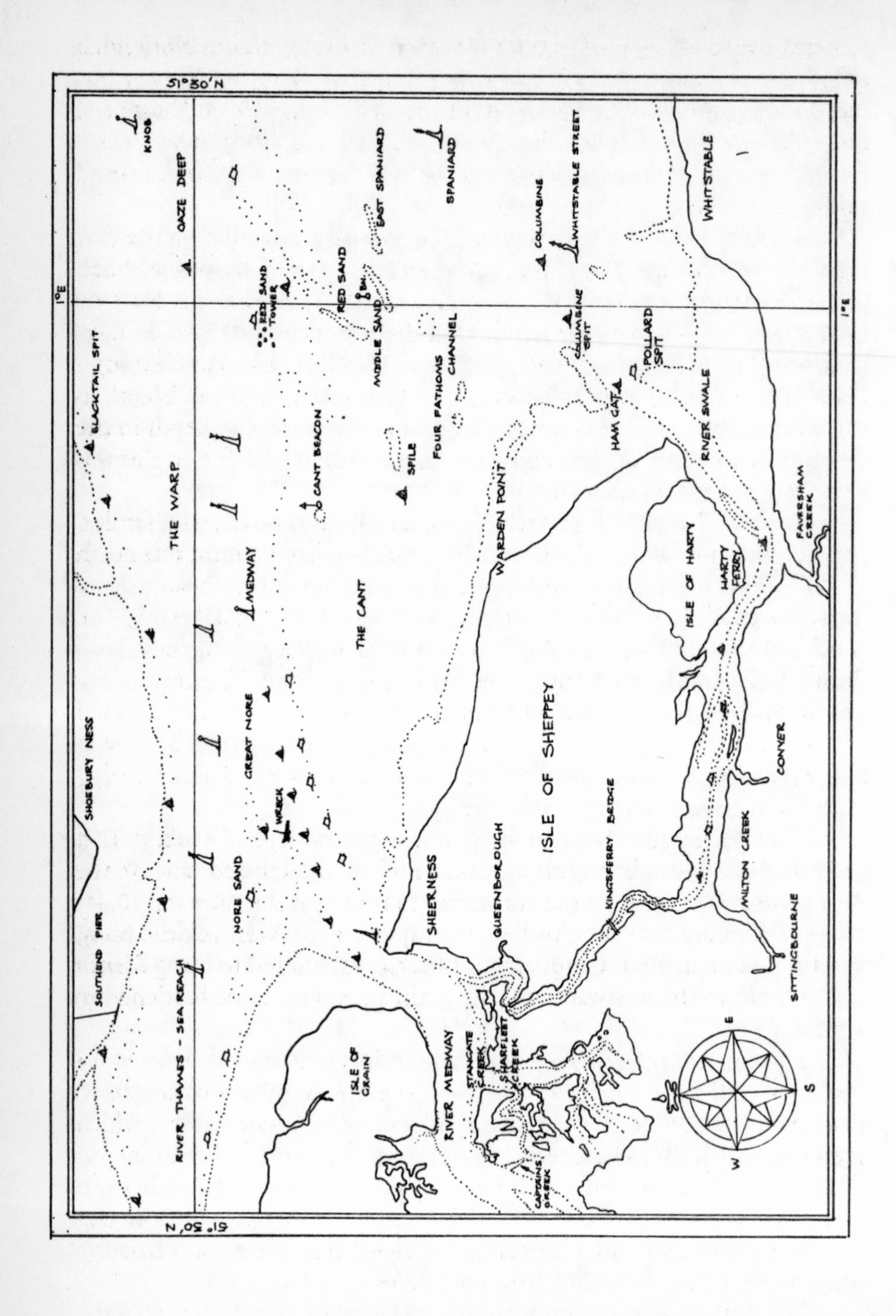
51°30'N
1°E
KNOB
OAZE DEEP
BLACKTAIL SPIT
THE WARP
SHOEBURY NESS
SOUTHEND PIER
RIVER THAMES - SEA REACH
NORE SAND
GREAT NORE
WRECK
MEDWAY
RED SAND TOWER
RED SAND
EAST SPANIARD
SPANIARD
MIDDLE SAND
CANT BEACON
THE CANT
SPILE
FOUR FATHOMS CHANNEL
COLUMBINE
WHITSTABLE STREET
COLUMBINE SPIT
POLLARD SPIT
HAM GAT
WHITSTABLE
RIVER SWALE
WARDEN POINT
ISLE OF HARTY
HARTY FERRY
FAVERSHAM CREEK
ISLE OF SHEPPEY
SHEERNESS
QUEENBOROUGH
KINGSFERRY BRIDGE
CONYER
MILTON CREEK
SITTINGBOURNE
ISLE OF GRAIN
RIVER MEDWAY
STANGATE CREEK
SHARFLEET CREEK
CAPTAINS CREEK
E
S
W

remembered our first visit to this spot when we met a famous Norwegian sailor named Rasmussen. He had sailed singlehanded from Norway but had gone aground on the Horse on the top of a spring tide and had been neaped there for about ten days. At the time I had found it very comforting that such an experienced sailor was making the same sort of mistakes that were troubling me.

Today however there were no problems with navigation on the first leg of this trip down to Shell Ness, and then on past the Columbine Shoal, as there is plenty of water in the channel which is well defined at low tide by the mud banks on either hand. Had the tide been full I would have been tempted to turn north about a mile past Shell Ness and pass through Ham Gat, a narrow gutway between the Columbine and the Island, as this would have saved us several miles, but at low water the depth in the Gat is only a couple of feet, and with *Merlin*'s draft of 5 ft 6 in this was obviously out of the question.

So we held our north-easterly course for another two and a half miles, and not until we reached the Columbine buoy which is almost due north of Whitstable did I dare to jibe her round to the north-north-west. Here we were a good three miles off the land and sailing on a broad reach. The wind was free, the sea was slight, and *Merlin* responded to these conditions by bounding along in a most satisfactory fashion. The noise of her bow wave increased, the rigging set up a continuous thrumming, and the end of the bowsprit pointed alternately at the sky and the sea. Mac, who had been curled up on the foredeck, came back to the cockpit having found that he was getting a trifle wet.

Time passes quickly when the sailing is enjoyable, and when we first picked up the South East Middle buoy, which marked the entrance to the Four Fathoms Channel, it was surprising to find that the time was 10.45. Fine on the port bow the children soon spotted the West Middle buoy, and for this we steered. Gradually our course was altered to bring *Merlin* round more to the westward and the main sheet had to be hardened in a trifle.

The coastline of Sheppey grew perceptibly nearer as we headed for Sheerness and the entrance to the river. There were only two dangers to beware of, the first being the remains of a war-time boom defence which projected out from the shore at Minster for about a mile. The other was Cheney Spit, a narrow strip of shingle extending for about two miles and over which there was a least depth of four feet at low water, but as we had now had about two and a half hours of flood tide there was obviously going to be plenty of water there for *Merlin*.

The breeze was certainly fresher than when we started and the thought of roaring up to Garrison Point where we should have to turn up into the wind right in the entrance was quite exciting. The Medway is still used by very large ships and we were approaching it from the east, absolutely blind. What I had forgotten was that as we neared the huge fort on the point we should temporarily be blanketed and would lose our wind, and had we met something big in the entrance, with no wind in our sails, we might have had difficulty in getting out of the way.

In the event we were lucky. The flood tide was carrying us strongly in and though we temporarily lost the wind and slowed down, as we glided past the fort the wind suddenly caught us again and we were off like a racehorse, heading straight for the mud on the Isle of Grain. There were four of us in the cockpit, together with Mac — and that small cockpit was never meant to take twelve feet! Fortunately there was no big ship trying to come out.

We just had time to put Mac down below before we reached the mud and I sang out 'Ready About!' Up went the helm, and on 'Lee-oh!' the children knew what to do: she came round like a bird and her head sails filled on the other tack. Here the tide was a boon for although I had to point her almost at the fort to get way on her, the flood was steadily sweeping us upstream. By the time we reached the shallows on the Sheerness side we were well clear of the fort, and when we went about again the next board was a long one that took us right over to the remains of Port Victoria. Another short board and we were almost at the entrance to Stangate Creek where we tacked and had a straight run up Saltpan Reach.

Kethole Reach was a bit difficult as the wind headed us, but the river is wide here and there was plenty of water. As we turned into Long Reach we roared away again and with the tide being now nearly full we were able to sail well over the Hoo Flats before tacking again up Pinup (pronounced 'Pine-up') Reach. This took us over to the Gillingham shore, just below the Strand, and then back on the port tack we had a breathing space and a clear run of over two miles up to the *Arethusa* at Upnor.

We had not been looking forward to the next part of our course, Chatham Reach, as this was two miles long and the wind was blowing almost straight down it. The tide also was slackening and was not much help, but there was nothing for it but to plug away, tack after tack, in the knowledge that once the tide turned against us our progress would be slower still. So we made the best of it and practised going about smartly. Much depended on the helmsman timing his shout of 'Lee-oh!' correctly, steering a correct course as she came round, and managing to shoot up into the eye of the wind without losing too much way. The crew of course had two head sails to worry about and theirs was the harder work, sheeting the sails in flat so that she pointed as high as possible. Though it was strenuous work there was satisfaction to be obtained in carrying it out efficiently, and it must be said that we all enjoyed it — even Mac, who recognized his home waters, and knew it would not be long before he was able to go ashore again.

At the top of Chatham Reach we were almost home and were able to relax. The wind was much lighter here in these sheltered waters, and in no time at all we were gliding alongside *Magnet* and making fast. Then on with the kettle and out with the fruit cake for a welcome mug of tea while we stowed the sails, cleaned up, and took Mac for his run.

6

A chapter of accidents

IF YOU believe, as some do, that misfortunes always come in threes, then listen to my tale of woe. For this is an account of how misfortune visited *Merlin* and her crew three several times: not three different mishaps but the same one, repeated on three occasions, and all because her skipper refused to learn a simple lesson, which is — never tow a dinghy at sea.

The first time I 'lost' a dinghy at sea was off Rottingdean, when sailing *Merlin* from Gosport to Sandwich. The dinghy came ashore a few days later further along the coast, and was recovered from the Receiver of Wrecks on payment of a modest fee. She was little the worse for her experience, and this should by rights have been enough to teach me the folly of trying to tow a dinghy in a heavy sea. But it did not.

The next time I 'lost' a dinghy — and the very same dinghy at that — was off the entrance to Calais harbour in a bit of a popple, and this time it cost me 3,000 francs. Anyone would think that to have to hand out 3,000 francs to a complete stranger in expiation of one's folly, and in front of one's wife and children, would be sufficiently shameful to cure a man of this particular foolishness. But even this was not enough. No, it had to happen a third time. It was in this wise.

We had spent a blissful two weeks cruising off the Essex coast, and exploring the rivers Colne and Blackwater from our favourite centre, Brightlingsea. The latter is, or was, the perfect place for a sailing holiday for anyone who likes 'messing about in boats'. There were many oyster smacks and Thames sailing barges about, as well as more modern yachts and sailing dinghies, and a good clean landing hard. The little town itself was full of life and character and all day long the water-front was busy with dinghies bustling to and fro. On the opposite side of the Colne estuary was Pyfleet Creek, a haven of peace protected by Mersea Island from the prevailing south-westerlies.

Because we were enjoying ourselves so much, and the weather was good, we prolonged our holiday until the last minute. With only two days to spare we decided to sail up the Blackwater to Maldon, which was *Merlin*'s port of registry. We beat several miles up the river, but then the sun went in, and the breeze became cold. So we turned past Osea Island and ran back to drop anchor in the sheltered reach off Stone, another delightful spot with a sandy beach and good bathing. But on our last day, when we should have been setting off across the Thames estuary back to the Kentish shore, the weather broke and we woke to find a cold, wet and miserable day with half a gale of wind blowing. Faced with the prospect of a long, uncomfortable sail home we gave in and returned home by train, leaving *Merlin* riding peacefully to her anchor and in the care of the local yacht club, who promised to keep an eye on her.

Our plan was to return the following weekend and sail her home, but when we left her we were not to know that we were in for a week of severe gales and torrential rain. For four days it blew and it rained as though the end of the world were coming, and when we went back to Stone the following Friday, though the wind had eased considerably, the countryside was cold and wet, and many branches had been blown off the trees.

There were three of us in the party, my son Anthony and I being accompanied by another good friend, Brian, who had sailed several times with us and knew *Merlin* well. We arrived at the yacht club late in the evening, looking forward to getting aboard and making an early start the following morning. Right up to the last minute we did not suspect that anything was amiss.

The club secretary was behind the bar when we went in and he greeted me in a rather strange way. He pulled a pint of beer, put it down on the bar in front of me, and said 'Drink that!' And not until I had downed over half of it would he give me the bad news that he had to break to us. In retrospect I do not think anyone could have done it in a nicer way.

Apparently during the gales *Merlin* had fouled her anchor and dragged across the river. She had grounded on a sandbank, had lain down on her side, and on the next tide had partly filled with water. Our good friends at the yacht club had fetched her back, pumped her out, and had even brought all the blankets ashore and washed them to get the salt out of them. These were still damp, and *Merlin* was of course pretty wet down below, so that nothing could be done until the morning. That night we slept at the yacht club and were more than grateful for their friendly hospitality.

Next morning we went out to investigate. If you have never seen the effect of turning a boat over on its side and filling it with salt water you will have difficulty in visualizing what we found. Notwithstanding quite a lot of cleaning up kindly undertaken by our friends at Stone who had helped with the salvage operations, the scene was still remarkable. For, as the ship had lain over, things had fallen off shelves, off bunks and out of lockers and had all been immersed together. We found bedding, blankets, marmalade, charts, sugar, cornflakes, a pack of playing cards, matches, clothes, a camera, even some treacle — all mixed up together and soaked in salt water. Never have I seen such a gooey, unwholesome mess, and it was difficult to know where to start.

However, we cleaned out the primus stoves — they also were full of water — lit them and set to work. All day Saturday, in intermittent rain, we spent drying out and clearing up, and by the evening we were exhausted but in a damp-dry condition. Also we were very hungry. Fortunately there was plenty of tinned food in the ship and we cooked ourselves an enormous meal, which made us feel very much more cheerful. We decided to leave on the ebb at six o'clock next morning, as this would just give us time to get out to the Spitway between the Gunfleet and Buxey sands while there was still enough depth of water to get through.

Sunday morning's weather was definitely wet and windy, but we got our anchor at 6.20 and proceeded downstream. With the tide under us and the wind almost dead aft we went like a train. Outside at sea, conditions were poor. It was rough, raining and the wind was very strong. We increased speed and *Merlin* sped through the grey, troubled waters like a mad thing. Visibility was sometimes only a few yards, sometimes half a mile. It was the fastest, wettest, most uncomfortable and most exhilarating sail ever. It did not last long.

The excitement of the ride caused me to forget the dinghy, which was planing behind us. Just as we were about to enter the Spitway I glanced aft casually to check that she was alright — and there she was, half full of water. At the speed we were travelling, the towing painter had

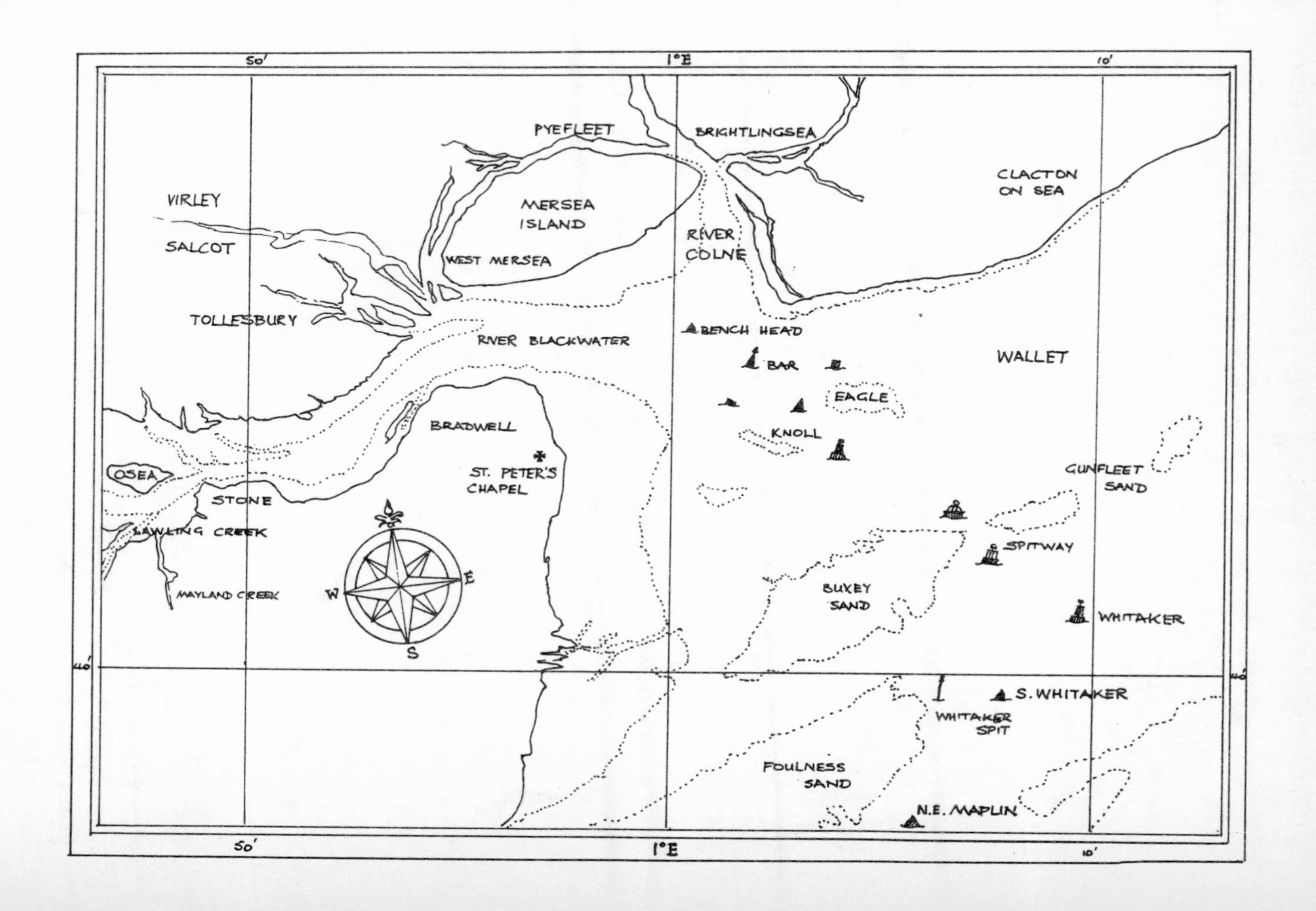
50'
1°E
10'
PYEFLEET
BRIGHTLINGSEA
CLACTON ON SEA
VIRLEY
MERSEA ISLAND
SALCOT
RIVER COLNE
WEST MERSEA
TOLLESBURY
BENCH HEAD
RIVER BLACKWATER
BAR
WALLET
EAGLE
BRADWELL
KNOLL
OSEA
ST. PETER'S CHAPEL
GUNFLEET SAND
STONE
LAWLING CREEK
SPITWAY
E
W
MAYLAND CREEK
BUXEY SAND
WHITAKER
S
40'
S. WHITAKER
WHITAKER SPIT
FOULNESS SAND
N.E. MAPLIN

pulled the bow right up and out of the water so that she was sitting well down on her stern. The force of the water under her had blown the top off the centre-board casing, and she had filled with water.

We pulled her alongside and just had time to get a warp round one of the thwarts before she sank. Then began the struggle to get her aboard *Merlin*. For a few moments all was confusion. The sea was rough, we were tearing through the water, and the waterlogged dinghy was a dead weight, impossible to manage and eagerly trying to trap our fingers against *Merlin*'s gunwale. It was obvious that we could do nothing while we were sailing so fast, so the first thing was to get *Merlin*'s sails off her. This made the job possible, though now we were wallowing about in a confused welter of grey water.

The Spitway buoy was in sight, so telling Anthony not to take his eye off it in case we drifted away, Brian and I tackled the dinghy. It was hard work and took longer than expected, but after an agonizing battle we managed to spill and bale enough water out of the dinghy to enable us to drag it over the gunwale and on to the deck. By the time it was safely secured we had drifted so far that the Spitway buoy was almost out of sight.

Very wet and uncomfortable we made sail again, but on account of the delay there was now no longer enough water for us to get through the channel between the sands. This meant a wait of several hours for the next flood tide, but by the time there was sufficient water for us to get through we would not then have had enough tide to carry us right up the Thames and into the Medway. The alternative was to call the whole thing off and beat back to Brightlingsea, and reluctantly we decided that this was the more sensible thing to do.

Rather dejectedly we turned and headed for the mouth of the Colne river. Land was out of sight and the grey heaving mass of sea that surrounded us was not the most inspiring of sights. But the fact that we had recovered the dinghy was a compensation, and during the next few hours I for one had plenty of time for contemplation, and for renewing the vow never to tow a dinghy at sea again.

It was two o'clock by the time we dropped anchor in a sheltered spot under the lee of Mersea Island. Suddenly the sun came out and it was gloriously warm. Thankfully we prepared a meal and stripped off our sodden clothes to dry.

We were still not out of trouble however.

After lunch we sailed over to Brightlingsea Creek and on the way, in a gust, the mainsail split from side to side. In spite of this Anthony brought *Merlin* up in masterly fashion to anchor between two other large yachts. Then he and Brian, after making a pair of makeshift oars (ours being lost when the dinghy sank), went ashore leaving me to start repairing the torn sail.

The next hour was the most unpleasant I ever spent in *Merlin*. When the wind was against the tide she had a nasty habit — due to her deep keel — of swinging round her anchor in a large circle. This she now started to do, pitching badly all the time, and I soon got worried about the yachts on either side as they were rather close. *Merlin* had a long and stout bowsprit which could do a lot of damage if it rammed anything while the ship was plunging up and down. The yacht on our left was a chromium-plated motor cruiser with no one aboard and *Merlin* seemed to take a dislike to it. I tried to restrain her by shortening in on the anchor chain: a fatal mistake, for the anchor dragged and before my very eyes she pranged the yacht. Fortunately I managed to jump aboard and make fast before she was able to do any serious damage. Eventually, Brian and Anthony returned to say they had arranged a quiet berth for us higher up the creek.

Once more we set sail, under very shortened sail, and were soon moored up in perfect peace. We tidied up and I got back to my sewing. Then came the final straw — I broke our only sail needle. We gave in and returned home!

The following weekend Anthony could not go, so only Brian and I went back to Brightlingsea. This time fortune smiled on us and there were no hitches. The weather was beautiful, the breeze was good, we caught the tide. The log opens with the entry: '11.30 cast off moorings, Brightlingsea Creek. Wind, moderate SE' and closes with '22.50 picked up mooring, Rochester, Kent.'

7

All good things . . .

JANUARY and February are bad months for yachtsmen. The boat is laid up, either in a mud berth or ashore, and visiting her only enhances the frustration at not being able to go for a sail. Also she looks terrible, shorn of all her beauty and dignity, her paintwork shabby, and down below is a damp, cold and unfriendly mess. Of course there is plenty to do ashore, what with rigging to be overhauled and renewed, navigation lights to be checked, blocks to be scraped and varnished, etc, but accompanying all these necessary and interesting tasks is a tremendous impatience to be off again.

One January I was passing through this particular phase, chafing at the weather, and wondering if spring was going to be early or late, even looking at my watch, subconsciously hoping that this might persuade the time to pass more quickly.

Actually, on one occasion glancing at my watch did have exactly this effect, for I chanced to see on the glass a big scratch mark, and this was enough to send me off into a daydream. The time was coming up to 3.15 pm when I saw the scratch on the glass, and as I was bored at the time the memory of how the scratch was incurred came flooding back. By rights I should not have been bored, for I was sitting in a committee meeting at work where we were considering the company's overheads, a subject in which I was normally very interested. But two of the accountants were arguing about a fairly obscure and minor point, and I lost interest. Also, I felt they were wasting our time because I already knew the answer!

But the sight of the scratched watch glass brought the scene vividly back to life. We were sailing a few miles out from Sheerness, somewhere near the Shivering Sands forts, and the sea was rather rough, a fairly familiar condition in this part of the Thames estuary where due to strong tides and many sandbanks the sea knocked up is often very short, steep and confused.

I had gone up forward to take in the staysail as she was pounding a bit in the head sea, and a fair amount of water was coming aboard. She

Mascotte

put her nose down into one wave larger than most and scooped up a great dollop of water that swept my legs from under me. Fortunately I had firm hold of the staysail halyard or I might have gone over the side, and all that happened was that I slithered across the deck and crashed into the anchor windlass. It would not have been surprising if the glass of my watch had been shattered, but in the event it was only scratched.

How long I was dreaming I don't really know, but I came back to reality in time to take part in the closing stages of the committee meeting, and no serious harm was done. But the incident served to set me thinking seriously of the coming season and the cruises we hoped to make. I was not to know at this time that this was to be the last season we should have in *Merlin*.

So we started planning for the summer, discussing what we proposed to do. Not that we were planning any dramatic voyages, or indeed anything of a dashing nature. No, our sailing was definitely of the 'messing about in boats' type, as I have said before, and we were quite happy pottering in and out of the Medway, with occasional jaunts across to the creeks of the Essex coast, and even to France, but all at our own pace and in our own choice of weather.

Our particular pleasure was to find a quiet anchorage in some sheltered creek where as the sun went down you were alone with the sea and the sky, and the only sounds were the lapping of the water against the hull of the boat and the last faint cries of the curlews and terns before they settled for the night. This was perfect bliss, and the finest possible therapy. In the mornings, soon after sunrise, the peace was equally heady, but with a difference, for at this hour there was always a feeling of expectancy in the air and the possibility of another wonderful day out in the open where we were our own masters, subject only to the influence of wind and tide.

Although *Merlin* was perfectly adequate for our needs there was no doubt she was a bit on the small side, and with only sitting headroom was a trifle cramped even for the four of us. And of course, four was really the maximum that we could sleep. So that it was with some surprise later on that we found ourselves planning a two-week holiday with no fewer than three guests. Of course it all happened quite gradually and casually, but with a degree of inevitability that was rather frightening.

To begin with, in addition to the four of us, or five if you count Mac, we now had a friend living with us on the good old sailing barge *Magnet*. Biddy was a teacher and a friend who used to visit us from time to time. One Sunday she came to tea and was obviously unwell, and by the time she was due to be rowed back ashore it was clear she was in no fit state for travel. So we put her to bed, and it was a full two weeks before she surfaced. After that it seemed logical for her to stay on, and she became a permanent member of the crew.

Now Biddy had a boyfriend who was in the army but was due to be demobbed. They had not seen each other for some considerable time but had corresponded regularly and had what at the time was called 'an understanding', or 'an arrangement'. So on his demobilization Geoff came down to stay with us and soon became a firm friend, and it was unthinkable that we should go on holiday without the pair of them. Hence the total ship's complement had increased to six, plus one dog. Finally, Anthony came home from school and asked permission to bring a friend, David, with us — and that made the party up to seven.

I must confess to having many misgivings about the wisdom of putting to sea with such a numerically swollen crew in such a small boat. There was absolutely nowhere where you could get away from people, and living in such close proximity for two weeks the odds on friction between members of the party were pretty high. Not one of us knew every other member of the crew before we set out, and poor David only knew Anthony — he must have wondered what on earth had hit him.

As it turned out there was no need to have worried. Everyone, including Mac, fitted in like pieces of a jigsaw puzzle and I don't think there was a single cross word spoken in the whole fortnight. Indeed we had one of the best — and certainly the most hilarious — holidays I can ever remember.

It is difficult to believe now how and where we all slept, but sleep we did, and enjoyed it. There were only two settee berths and these were occupied by my wife and Biddy. Two of the children slept in the fo'c'sle and the other on the cabin sole between the two settees. We slung a large tarpaulin over the boom, which created a very good cabin for Mac in the cockpit — in fact he had more room than any of us — and Geoff and I slept on the coachroof under the tarpaulin.

The coachroof had a bit of a camber on it, which tended to slide you to one side, and it by no means provided a flat and unimpeded surface on which to lie. Indeed on my side, the starboard side, there were three wooden chocks screwed to it, these normally holding a lifebuoy. What Geoff had to contend with I cannot remember, but rather fancy that on the port side were the rails on which the main hatch slid when opened. But it didn't seem to matter very much — perhaps we were so exhausted by the time we turned in that we could have slept anywhere.

We were certainly helped by the weather, which though not perfect, was pretty kind to us. There was some rain, though not enough to dampen our spirits, and I remember one anxious night when it blew hard, and outside on the coachroof it sounded worse than it was. We were in Queenborough on a mooring, and in the grey light of dawn, in intermittent driving rain, a small yacht nearby dragged her anchor and ultimately bumped alongside us. I can still recall lifting the edge of our improvized tent from time to time and seeing this wretched boat coming nearer and nearer, and willing its anchor to hold before it reached us so that I did not have to get out of my warm sleeping bag and do something about it. But it was no use, and ultimately both Geoff and I had to get up and go out in the rain and moor the boat alongside.

We did not go very far on this holiday, but visited all our favourite haunts in the Medway and Swale — Stangate and Half Acre Creeks, Lower Halstow, and Harty Ferry, Oare Creek, and we sailed out to the Nore and round the North Foreland to Ramsgate, which had always been a favourite port of call since the time we lived in Sandwich.

The time passed all too quickly and it was a very reluctant crew who wended their way back up the Medway towards Rochester. On the last evening before we were due to get back to our mooring alongside *Magnet*, Geoff (who had been a tower of strength on this holiday) planned a farewell dinner, and Anthony became his assistant chef.

So we dropped anchor in Cockham Reach, just below Upnor, and because space aboard *Merlin* was so restricted the two chefs sent all the rest of us ashore while they prepared the meal. This took some time, and while we patiently waited we were occasionally intrigued by the sight of one or other of them climbing out of the fore hatch and running round to disappear down the main. Later we discovered that they were so short of space in laying things out that they had to institute a one-way traffic route.

However, the result was well worth waiting for, and was a remarkable achievement considering that they were cooking for seven on two ordinary Primus stoves. Geoff is also a talented artist and had produced an illustrated and decorated Menu card in 'French', headed 'Salon de Squashé: Le Dejeuner Annual de la Cruise Merlin. Chef: M. Geofant.' This listed no fewer than nine courses, and a number of toasts. The Menu has survived and is reproduced herewith.

This was indeed the last holiday we were to have in *Merlin*, and Geoff's 'Salon de Squashé' dinner was a fitting climax to several years happy cruising. It was some months later before we actually parted with her, and like so many of the major events in one's life it came about casually and apparently accidentally.

One day two young Australians came aboard *Magnet* to see me. They had seen *Merlin* about in the river and had taken a liking to her and wanted to buy her. I explained that she was not for sale, but they had got the bug badly and were not to be put off. We haggled a bit, but not for very long, for they were determined to have her, and agreed to pay a figure which I regarded as very reasonable indeed. Perhaps I was hard up at the time.

I well remember the night they called to pay for her, and to be given the Certificate of Registry. We sat round the table in *Magnet*'s saloon in the gentle light of the oil lamp, and they carefully counted out several hundred rather grubby pound notes, and I must say that this pile of money on the table did ease the pangs of parting just a little. The following day when I came home from work she had gone.

There is a sequel to this story — a two-part sequel in fact. At fitting out time next spring one of the Australians came back and asked for the name of the marvellous paint I had used on *Merlin*'s bottom, for though it was obviously an expensive one they wanted to use none other. I had to admit that in fact it was ordinary gasworks tar, that had cost me all of 1/6d per gallon. We subsequently saw *Merlin* once or twice on our travels in the Medway area, and often wondered what ultimately became of her. One day some years later we found out.

We were in Queenborough again, and walked up the side of the

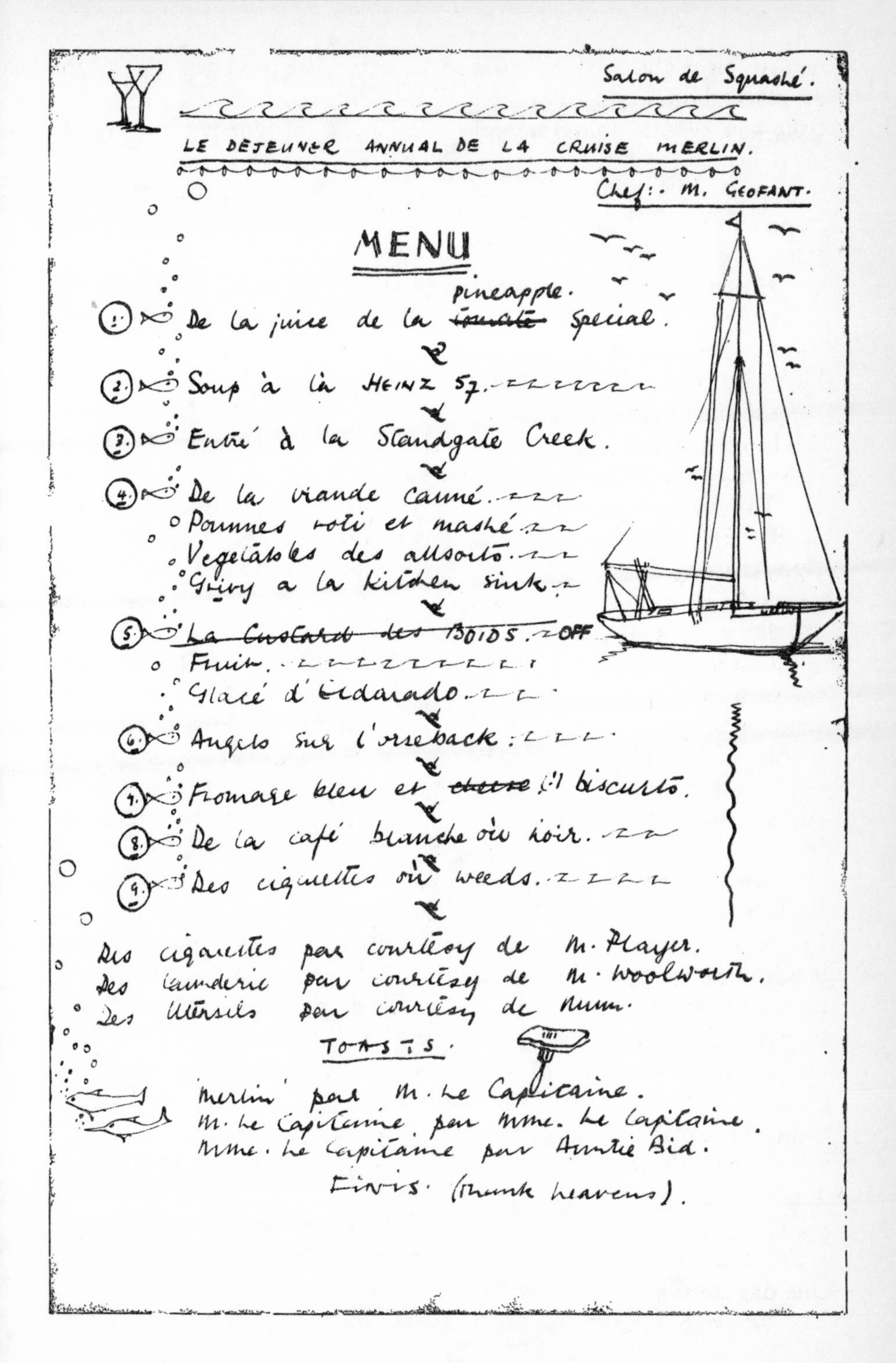

Salon de Squashé.

LE DEJEUNER ANNUAL DE LA CRUISE MERLIN.

Chef:- M. GEOFANT.

MENU

1. De la juice de la ~~tomato~~ pineapple special.
2. Soup à la HEINZ 57.
3. Entré à la Standgate Creek.
4. De la viande canné.
   Pommes roti et mashé.
   Vegetables des allsorts.
   Gravy a la kitchen sink.
5. ~~La Custard des Boids.~~ OFF
   Fruit.
   Glacé d'Eldarado.
6. Angels sur l'orseback.
7. Fromage bleu et ~~cheese~~ 'l biscuits.
8. De la café blanche ou noir.
9. Des cigarettes ou weeds.

Des cigarettes par courtesy de M. Player.
Des laundrie par courtesy de M. Woolworth.
Des Utensils par courtesy de Mum.

TOASTS.

Merlin par M. Le Capitaine.
M. Le Capitaine par Mme. Le Capitaine.
Mme. Le Capitaine par Auntie Bid.

Finis. (thank heavens).

creek that wends its way up through the town. At the top of the creek were a number of old boats, most of which had reached the end of their useful lives. Among them was *Merlin*, half full of water, derelict and abandoned, and it was a sight I wish I had not seen. I remembered old Harry Feltham's remark in Portsmouth when I bought her:

'She will outlive you' he had said — but he had been wrong.

PART 2

GRAYLING

Sail forth into the sea, O ship!
Through wind and wave, right onward steer!
The moistened eye, the trembling lip
Are not the signs of doubt or fear!

LONGFELLOW

8

A fish is hooked

I FIRST saw the auxiliary sloop *Grayling* on a bright and breezy Saturday afternoon in July 1954. I was in a state of suspended animation at the time; that is to say, I was without a boat, having sold my 7-ton cutter *Merlin* about six months previously in the mistaken belief that I could live without her. Once the thrill of having in my hands nearly £400 in grubby pound notes had worn off — it lasted exactly eleven days — I realized my mistake and once more took to reading the classifieds in the yachting magazines.

From then on, every Saturday, with a friend to help me, I went looking at boats. Brian was as upset as I that *Merlin* had been sold, and was missing his sailing more than somewhat, and from this point of view he acted as a spur to my enthusiasm and not as a brake, which was a pity. There were several occasions when — with the voice of the tempter in my ear — I nearly bought an unsuitable boat.

One of these was a boat we found in Christchurch harbour. She had rakish lines, a clipper bow, and a romantic name, which I think was *Blue Seas*. Her length was about 25 ft, there was standing headroom down below, and a strip of carpet on the cabin sole. What her draft was I shudder to think, for when you stepped aboard she was so tender as to suggest an imminent capsize. But the great attraction from Brian's point of view was a really gorgeous bit of stuff who was the friend of the owner and his wife. I explained to him that the girl did not go with the boat, but if she had then I think I should have been pressurized into doing a deal.

Come July we had still not found a boat, and travelled down one Saturday afternoon to Wallasea Bay on the River Crouch to look at a converted fishing smack which sounded a possibility. The boatman picked us up in his launch and took us out through the moorings to the boat we had come to see. Even before we climbed aboard I knew it was hopeless, but the boatman was on his way somewhere else and said he would pick us up on his way back. Five minutes was enough to convince both of us that this was not the boat, she had been very roughly converted

by a not very competent DIY enthusiast, and had been liberally daubed with bright blue paint. I like old boats, but not 'ole tore-outs'.

Rather dejectedly, back on deck we sat down on the coach roof to await the boatman's return and casually glanced round the moorings. It was a lovely afternoon with a blue sky and a few fleecy white clouds, and the wind was southerly, force 2-3. As we sat there the only sounds were the frapping of halyards and the lapping of water against countless hulls.

There were seemingly hundreds of boats on the moorings, of all shapes and sizes, and some were very beautiful. One particularly stood out, an obvious thoroughbred, slightly larger than those around her, perhaps 40 ft overall, and with an enormously tall mast. We both commented on her beautiful lines, sighed wistfully at the thought of owning such an obviously expensive yacht, and looked away.

As we climbed back into the launch and sped away from the bright blue fishing boat, without a backward glance, I mentioned the thoroughbred and said what a beautiful boat she was.

'She's for sale,' said the boatman, 'Come and have a look at her.'

'No' I said, 'It's a waste of time. She is a gentleman's yacht, and way outside my range.'

But by this time he had altered course, and very soon we drew up alongside.

She had guard rails. Galvanized iron stanchions and twin wire guard rails. I had never even been on a yacht with guard rails before. As Brian and I simultaneously swung ourselves aboard she did not roll. There was no movement, none at all, and my heart filled with awe. I subsequently discovered the reason for this — she drew 6 ft 9 in.

The decks were broad enough to walk right round, without tripping over anything, the trim was teak, she was old but very beautiful. I looked up at the mast — 56 ft 4½ in from deck to truck — and shuddered at all its rigging, being used only to simple shrouds and cross trees, back stays and a forestay. Down below she was panelled in mahogany. Yes, panelled!

As a matter of interest I asked the price. This was £1,100, almost twice the £600 which was the maximum I could scrape together. £600 may not sound very much today in view of our debased currency, but nearly forty years ago, to me, it was a fortune. Sadly, but having enjoyed the experience, we expressed our thanks and went home.

On Monday morning, having forgotten all about her, I was sitting in my office, earning my bread and butter, when my secretary rang through.

'There's a Mr Albert Ogle wishes to speak to you' she said. She put him through and a quiet voice with a north country accent said:

'Good morning Mr Winter. My name is Albert Ogle, and I'm a timber merchant in Grimsby. I believe you looked at my boat *Grayling* on Saturday, and liked her.'

I agreed with him that this was nothing but the truth, but not the whole truth, and expressed sorrow that he had been falsely led to believe that I was a possible customer.

'Make me an offer, Mr Winter' said Mr Ogle.

'Mr Ogle' I replied, 'I couldn't even make you an offer that would not insult you. She is a beautiful boat, but way, way outside my price range.'

And that was that. We had a very pleasant chat about boats in general, and about *Grayling* in particular, and he rang off. The next day the telephone rang again.

'I've been thinking' said Albert Ogle, 'How about £950?'

Sadly I reiterated my arguments of yesterday.

On Wednesday he said '£750?' And though I still said 'No' it was a little less firmly.

On Thursday he rang again.

'I'll tell you what, Mr Winter,' he said quietly, 'You meet me at Wallasea Bay on Sunday, and we'll have a little sail together.'

'Oh, Mr Ogle' I said, desperately looking round for straws to clutch. 'And I know what will happen. And so do you.'

'Well, we'll see' he said, with a smile in his voice.

Sunday was a glorious day. When Brian and I arrived at Wallasea Bay it was to find a cold luncheon awaiting us in *Grayling*'s mahogany-panelled saloon. A lunch of very high quality, impeccably served. We could have been in the Ritz. It was a most unfair act of salesmanship.

After lunch we got sail on her and left the mooring, and in that narrow crowded river, full of weekend yachtsmen, he let me take her. Perhaps he knew that the fish was now hooked, and that all that was needed was that little twitch of the line to make sure he did not get away.

Grayling handled superbly, and to sail her in these crowded waters was a joy. When we returned to the mooring Albert Ogle and I repaired to the saloon to talk business. Fortunately I had remembered to bring my cheque book. He seemed happy with the deal, and there was no doubt in my mind that I was getting value for money. The many subsequent happy years spent in *Grayling* amply confirmed this opinion.

★ ★ ★

Grayling's vital statistics were interesting, and to me slightly awe-inspiring. Her length overall was 37 ft 6 in, her beam 9 ft, and her draught 6 ft 9 in. She had large overhangs, her waterline length being 28 ft 6 in. She had been built in 1900 of good materials by Stone Brothers Ltd, of Brightlingsea in Essex. Originally a yawl, her rig had been cut down to sloop in 1908, and later a new mast measuring over 56 ft from the deck had given her a fairly hefty Bermudan mainsail. Her performance on the wind was excellent, her hull shape being somewhat similar to the fish after which she had been named. She was fast, making little fuss through the water, and was very, very wet.

I never ceased to wonder at how she slipped through the water leaving apparently no wake. Even at high speed it was as if the water just closed round her, and many people remarked on this. Because of her deep draught there was no need for a coach roof, and she was flush decked. There were two large skylights, the after one of which was immediately forward of the cockpit and was covered with a useful grid seat. The cockpit was self-draining and shallow, and provided no shelter at all from the elements. In fact, if there was any weather about you just sat out in it.

Down below there was a considerable degree of comfort, with standing headroom throughout. The forepeak was large, with plenty of stowage for sails and warps, etc, and even for one person to sleep at a pinch. Then came the galley and loo, both of which were small, but adequate. A step down brought you into the saloon which was very well appointed with two full-length settee berths, which were upholstered in a green uncut moquette, a sideboard and drinks cupboard, bookshelves, etc, and a full-length hanging cupboard. Aft of the saloon was the main hatch and then two very comfortable and wide bunks with drawers under. At the end of these two berths, and between them, was the navigating table which when taken out revealed the engine. Altogether a very civilized and satisfactory layout, allowing four people to cruise in comfort. Having been used to the rather cramped conditions in *Merlin* we regarded *Grayling*'s accommodation as little short of palatial.

In 1929, while engaged in the North Sea Race, she had had the misfortune to be dismasted in a bit of a blow, and this necessitated a rescue operation by the Harwich-Hook of Holland ferry. Unfortunately, while the ferry was alongside and they were sorting things out, both ships were rolling badly and the ferry's huge rubbing strake came down on *Grayling*'s deck and did a considerable amount of damage. This was later repaired and was not discernible to the casual eye, but it certainly left her with a weakness.

Another structural weakness was in her long counter where the rudder trunking was extremely difficult to maintain, and neglect by a succession of owners over the years had left this in a leaking condition which was a perpetual source of trouble. Several wise and well-meaning friends advised me to saw off the counter, which even in the 1950s was regarded as old fashioned and effete, but I could never bring myself to commit such an act of vandalism. It would have spoilt her lines completely. The best palliative we found was to pour hot pitch down the trunking from time to time, an expedient which may cause the purists to shudder, but which certainly diminished the leak.

On 27 August 1954 Brian and I, with another colleague, travelled to Wallasea Bay to take possession of *Grayling*, and bring her home to Rochester where we were still living aboard *Magnet*. The ship's log has the following entry:

> Arrived Wallasea Bay to take over *Grayling* 8.30 pm. Brian Driscoll, Bert Guest, and C.W.R.W. Anthony arrived from Mistley at 11.00 pm, having thumbed a lift from Burnham-on-Crouch.

My son Anthony was sixteen years old at the time. He had recently left Sir Roger Manwood's School in Sandwich, and had gone to sea. Our arrangements for meeting him in Burnham that evening went very sadly astray, and though Brian rowed over in the dinghy and spent a considerable time searching for him it was to no avail, and he had to return without him. It appears that they both did a tour of the pubs and made enquiries, but never managed to meet. Anthony subsequently turned up in style in a very smart motor launch, the tender to some very large yacht, and driven by a rather splendid military-looking owner and his wife in faultless yachting attire, who seemed pleased to have been of service. We have long since ceased to wonder where Anthony found this seeming ability always to land on his feet. It was very late that night when we turned in, there was so much that was new and exciting to explore in *Grayling*, and it was a very tired but happy crew who flopped into their bunks in the early hours.

Partly as a consequence of our very late night we made a leisurely start the following morning, and it was in fact 12.40 before we dropped the mooring and proceeded downstream under engine. The weather was if anything too perfect, bright hot sunshine with very little wind, but nothing could lessen the thrill of putting to sea in such a magnificent boat. While the others hauled out all the sails there were, and experimented with different combinations, the new owner sat at the tiller in a state of advanced bliss. The log records that the journey across the Thames estuary to the Medway took around 10½ hours, with the engine running practically all the time, and that it was precisely at 23.00 hours that we dropped our anchor in Stangate Creek.

Stangate Creek is one of the delights of the lower Medway, and a very firm favourite of ours. Situated not far from Sheerness and the entrance to the River Swale it offers a deep water but sheltered anchorage, and in those days complete peace and tranquility. At the top of the Creek, which dries at low water, is the charming village of Lower Halstow where there is a delightful Saxon church, a pub, a shop, and a public telephone — all the things a yachtsman needs after a spell at sea.

The trip over from Burnham taught us little about *Grayling*'s sailing properties, but confirmed that at least the engine was easy to start and would keep running quietly for several hours. The engine — a Morris 'Navigator' — was very easy of access, and the chart table light was so placed that it illuminated the engine when work had to be carried out.

What this initial voyage did not tell us was that there were two problems connected with this engine that were destined to cause us considerable trouble in the years to come. One was that the exhaust, which was short and came out under the counter, was very close to the water level, so that in a seaway it was possible for water to find its way back into the engine. This happened frequently and it proved to be very difficult, because of the position of the self-draining cockpit, to provide an adequate U-bend to prevent this happening.

The other problem concerned the petrol supply which came from a copper tank housed in a teak locker on deck. This suffered from two major faults, the first being that the tank was continually forming a rather nasty green gunge in the petrol, and as soon as she started bouncing about this got churned up and was sucked down the feed pipe into the carburettor. We were for ever having to clean this out, but never cured the fault and ultimately had to scrap the tank in favour of a fibreglass one built to fit the tank locker.

The second fault with the petrol supply, which was also cured by scrapping the tank, was that the outlet from it was on the port end (the tank lay athwartships) with the result that when she was heeled over on the port tack the engine suffered fuel starvation, particularly when the petrol level was low. The log contains several references to this complaint in the form of the initials 'P.T.F.E.' 'P.T.F.E.' is a well know silicone product used in engineering, but as far as *Grayling* was concerned it stood for Port Tack Fuel Economy!

These troubles however were very minor compared to the joy of sailing *Grayling*, and the fun she gave us and our friends. Anthony only saw her in the times when he was at home, and ultimately Sally went away to school, but she was able to get in some sailing in the holidays. However we had several friends who were regular members of her crew, particularly Brian, who had helped to find her; Pat, who became the most important crew member; and Geoff, whose romance with Biddy never fruited, but who came on several cruises with us together with Monk, a friend of his, who was a skilled engineer and an invaluable companion. When Geoff and Monk were aboard there were not many dull moments.

As in all departments in life it is the quality of one's friends that count, and in this respect both *Grayling* and her owner were especially blessed.

9

A sunset sail

ONCE having taken possession of *Grayling*, and having brought her back safely to her new home port of Rochester, it was not long before we were itching to be off again. We had several short sails up and down the Medway with various admiring friends, all of whom were eager to sample our new toy, and I have no doubt that we swanked a bit. But within three weeks Brian and I had both managed to wangle a few days leave, and we were off.

'Where shall we go?' said Brian.

'Well, we don't want to go mad. We've only a few days, so we can't go far. How about going down the North Kent coast to Ramsgate?'

'Sounds alright to me. When do we start?'

As we dropped down the river on the ebb the breeze was light and fluky and really the tide was doing more to propel us than the wind. But it was extremely peaceful and relaxing, and as we stowed things away and made ourselves comfortable we spoke quietly. Down Chatham Reach the dockyard on our right was quiet and still, the day's work over, and across the marshes to our left Strood was silhouetted against the evening sky on which the colours of sunset were beginning to build up.

There were very few naval ships moored in Chatham Reach, but I remembered the occasion in 1952 when this stretch of water was crowded with warships from all the countries of the world, all visiting England to honour and celebrate the coronation of Her Majesty Queen Elizabeth II. We had sailed down the river one day then with the children, recognizing this navy and that navy from their ensigns, until Sally happened to spot the Indian and Pakistan visitors ships, one ensign of which contained a representation of a huge elephant.

'Look, Daddy,' she had said, 'Fremlin's navy!' Fremlins was a local Kent brewery whose trademark was an elephant.

But this evening the river was quiet and we had it to ourselves. At Upnor, where the river almost does a U-bend to the right we glided silently past the training ship *Arethusa*, her riding lights already burning,

and her tall spars showing black against the paling sky. In Cockham Reach the woods come right down to the waters edge, and the yacht moorings here belonging to the Medway Yacht Club are as beautiful as any in the country.

Lower down this reach, off Hoo, were rows of moorings occupied by moth-balled warships, ships of all shapes and sizes, from destroyers down to some extraordinarily ugly craft sprouting forests of stove pipes. These were all numbered with the suffix LBK, and must surely have had some culinary connection, though we never discovered what this was. Biddy, however, decided that the letters must stand for 'Lovely Big Kitchens'.

It was in this area, alongside a moored frigate or some such, that Anthony had earned his spurs some years previously as a small boy. He had been taking part in a childrens' race in Hoo Regatta, in a class of small single-handed dinghies which had a rather elementary Una-rig. These boats were safe enough but were difficult to tack, and he got into stays and went bumping alongside one of the warships. His slightly anxious father was watching through binoculars and saw the club's safety boat rush to his assistance, only to be waved away by a furious Anthony who was quite confident of being able to extricate himself from the mess he had got into. These are the little incidents that one remembers gratefully years later, and which were described so neatly in the lyric of a popular song of the day as 'forget-me-nots in life's bouquet'.

As we passed down Pinup Reach and rounded Darnet Ness the sun had already sunk below the horizon, and the sky was filled with that magical afterglow which softens and romanticizes the landscape. The ruins of the old Napoleonic fort on the Ness were standing stark and stern above the marsh, and the tide had already dropped far enough for some of the 'farmer's teeth' to be showing. These 'farmer's teeth' were a common sight on the Medway — stakes driven into the mud to limit erosion of the river bank — but they certainly gave the impression that they were there to prevent anyone landing on the marsh. They were particularly thick round Darnet Ness, which is an island at high tide, and can on good tides be left to port by shoal-draught craft passing down the river, which can thus pass through into South Yantlet Creek and Half Acre Creek. But these were no waters for *Grayling* with her deep draught, and we proceeded gently on our way down the dredged channel which is well buoyed and lit.

In due course we arrived at the entrance to our chosen anchorage for the night, Stangate Creek. Giving Stangate Spit a wide berth on our starboard hand, for we knew it stretched out well into the main river to trap the unwary, we turned to starboard into the creek and glided gently in the stillness for the next mile or so, until with mutual accord, and almost without speaking, we decided that this was far enough, and that here was as peaceful a spot as could be found in which to spend the night.

It was the work of only a few minutes to set up the topping lift, lower the jib and mainsail, and secure the latter to the boom with tyers. The anchor was let go in about 2½ fathoms, three times this length of chain being paid out, and the riding light was lit and hoisted on the forestay. When everything was ship-shape we had a last quick look round, noting with satisfaction the well-known landmarks around us — the lights on the oil refinery on the Isle of Grain, and the loom of the lights from the Medway towns on the horizon — and then we went down below.

We blinked as we switched on the light, and smiled at each other, for our little holiday break had begun well. Now for a drink and some food!

★ ★ ★

One of the irritating things about English weather is the rapidity with which it can change. The evening had been calm and peaceful, but during the night the glass dropped, and the morning broke cold and grey with a thin, biting wind. While the kettle was boiling I poked my head out of the hatch and surveyed the scene, which was pretty bleak. The sky was grey, the water was grey, even the marshes looked grey, and the creek was deserted.

However, the first mug of hot tea cheered us both up, and it was not long before we were shaved, washed, dressed, and ready for the day. Brian volunteered to cook the breakfast, and as there were no other volunteers he got the job. And it was while he was doing it that a cry came from the galley.

'Hey, Skipper, I can't find any coffee!'

Then of course I remembered that we had drunk the last of the coffee the week before, and it had not been replaced.

'Never mind, we can call at Queenborough on the way out and buy some there. And anything else we have forgotten.'

So, after the breakfast things had been cleared away and stowed we got sail on her, raised and stowed the anchor, and in the smartish breeze that was blowing were soon bowling down the creek in fine style. Out in the main river we turned to starboard and with freed sheets went storming along towards Queenborough Spit, round which we gybed to enter the Swale. It was not until we gybed that we appreciated the strength in the wind. It was beginning to blow much harder.

'Wind seems to be freshening' I shouted as we hardened in the sheets, and *Grayling* heeled over and went charging up the Swale towards the Queenborough anchorage.

'At least it will keep the rain off.'

As we were not intending to stay very long we went alongside a loaded cement lighter moored just below the town hard, and Brian, complete with shopping list, jumped into the dinghy and rowed off. He had not been gone long before another boat came into the anchorage, a smart looking converted MFV called *Jenny May* whose owner I knew. We greeted each other.

'Where are you bound?' he enquired.

'Ramsgate — for a couple of days.'

'Have you heard the weather forecast this morning? It's bad. Sou-westerly gale on its way. I would hang on for a bit and see what happens if I were you.'

'Thanks. You may be right. There's no doubt the wind is getting up a bit. Though we've only got a few days and don't want to waste them in port.'

He waved and went on his way, up the river to his mooring in Strood. When Brian returned we discussed what to do.

'Someone in the grocer's shop told me the same thing,' he said. 'The next 24 hours is going to be all wind and rain.'

'OK then, I suppose we'd better be prudent. Let's wait until tomorrow morning, we have a nice sheltered mooring here, and there are plenty of little jobs we can do on the boat.'

A gleam came into Brian's eye.

'I know one job I want to do — give the cooker a good clean, it hardly had enough go in it to cook the breakfast this morning.'

So it became a make do and mend day, and before long Brian had the two-burner Calor gas stove in bits all over the saloon, while I put on an extra sweater and went out on deck to reeve a new burgee halyard. This job took less time than expected, for I had anticipated problems in getting the new line through the sheaf at the top of the mast, but in fact having spliced an end of the new on to the old, it rove through fairly easily, and our Little Ship Club burgee was soon fluttering away bravely at the mast head.

Brian's efforts with the stove were also crowned with success, and indeed he was so fired with enthusiasm for cooking that he immediately set about making a shepherd's pie for lunch. The success of this pie, which was delicious, spurred him on to even greater efforts, and he announced his intention of going ashore again to get something special for the evening meal. Obviously this had to be encouraged, for any expertise expended in the galley department benefited the whole ship's company, and as a reluctant cook it had my full support.

So we sallied forth together into the town, and returned to the ship loaded with goodies, both solid and liquid, designed to make our stay in Queenborough as pleasant as possible. The ship's log records that this object was satisfactorily achieved, for that night we dined in style, the menu comprising chicken noodle soup, lamb chops with saute potatoes and green peas, followed by apricots and cream, and a little Stilton. The meal was preceded by a glass of sherry, and accompanied by a bottle of Niersteiner Domtal.

As we sat over our coffee and after-dinner mints, and finished off the bottle of wine, and the gale force wind howled outside in the rigging, *Grayling* trembled slightly in the gusts and we found it hard to regret that we had not gone to sea in the morning and spent a wet and windy day on passage to Ramsgate. In fact we even felt a little smug at the way the day had turned out, though as we looked round at *Grayling*'s beautiful mahogany-panelled bulkheads glowing warmly in the lamplight we were consciously grateful that we were able to relax and enjoy ourselves in such comfort.

You meet all sorts when you are sailing. As we were getting ready to leave Queenborough in the morning a small motor cruiser came fussing up the river and slowed down as she came alongside. The man at the wheel said quietly:

'Excuse me, but can we get a train to town from Queenborough? Or is there a bus service to Sittingbourne?'

While we were telling him where the station was, and explaining the position of the landing hard, suddenly his hatch opened and the top half of a man popped out, rather like a Jack-in-the-box. He was faultlessly attired in black coat and striped trousers and was wearing a bowler hat. Though we were no more than three or four feet away from him, and in the middle of a conversation with his colleague, he shouted at the top of his voice the one word:

'Queenborough?'

and almost before we had time to reply disappeared below — presumably to pick up his briefcase. The man at the wheel smiled apologetically at us, thanked us for our help, and the motor cruiser slid away towards the hard. Presumably he had a train to catch.

The weather had improved considerably, and though the glass was still low and more gales were threatened, there did not seem to be any reason why we should not make the comparatively short trip to Ramsgate. The plan was to leave more or less on the top of the tide so that we would carry the ebb all the way to the North Foreland, by which time the south going stream would be running strongly past Broadstairs and Ramsgate. There is nothing like letting the tide work for you. Also by leaving near high water we would have the maximum depth on the early part of the trip as we crossed the Cant, which is a huge shallow area stretching for several miles off the Isle of Sheppey.

The buoyed big ship channel into the Medway from the Thames has a least depth of 25 ft, but to the eastward of this the Cant lies like a large plateau and some of the figures on the chart are frightening, with patches carrying as little as 4 ft depth even a mile from the shore. When you have a boat under you needing about 7 ft it behoves you to take care.

Another hazard just outside Sheerness that has to be remembered is the wreck of the *Richard Montgomery* which still lies on the edge of the deep water channel. This is a World War 2 ship loaded with ammunition and high explosives that was sunk just before she reached Sheerness and has been there ever since, constituting a perpetual threat to shipping, and indeed to Sheerness itself. The experts say that her cargo is still far too dangerous to approach, and that if anything triggered off an explosion the blast would blow Sheerness off the face of the earth. So she remains unmolested, and has to be given a wide berth by all and sundry.

Grayling's log records our departure very simply:

11.05 Cast off mooring, Queenborough. Light S.E. breeze.
11.45 Garrison Point abeam. Breeze slightly fresher. Making good progress.

Once we were clear of Sheerness harbour our course was east-north-east parallel with the line of buoys marking the deep water channel, but after making a suitable offing to avoid the shallowest part of the Cant we changed course to the east, heading for the Spile Buoy marking the entrance to the Four Fathoms Channel. This is a channel — so called because it has a depth of four fathoms at high water — which runs in an easterly direction skirting the south side of the Spile and Middle Sands, and marked in those days by a line of buoys some of which were only a mile or so apart and were like a well signposted road.

The last buoy in the row was the Spaniard, and from here our course turned slightly southerly towards the Horse Channel and the West Last buoy, five miles away. This buoy was a critical one for us for it marked a narrow gap between two sandbanks, and this was a gap we had to find or risk piling ourselves up on the Margate Hook Sands. The breeze was freshening all the time and beginning to head us, and Brian who was on the tiller was having difficulty in laying a correct course. I was happy to relieve him of this responsibility for this was my first experience of sailing *Grayling* in a stiff breeze, and I was delighted with the way she handled. We hardened in the jib sheet as much as possible, and soon found the setting of the main sheet that she liked best, and I discovered that in the gusts it was possible to luff up into the wind and make several yards to windward each time. By this means we managed to claw our way out of danger and went racing past the West Last buoy and into the channel between the sands.

The speed with which this buoy dropped astern was very satisfying and showed just how fast we were travelling. Here we were fairly close inshore, not much more than a mile from Reculver, the ruined twin church towers of which showed up very clearly, but from now on we were in rapidly deepening water and navigation was less of a problem. On our starboard hand the coastline was slipping past, and to port was a great expanse of water, though much of this was treacherously shallow and hid the long range of Margate Sands which lie parallel with the coast. Only half a mile away on our port side we passed the lonely Margate Hook Beacon, a tall post with an inverted cone topmark, standing in the midst of the grey water, but which in a few hours time would be high on the drying sands. Not a place for the *Graylings* of this world to linger for long.

As it strengthened the wind was veering southerly, and for the next two hours we went roaring along this north Kent coast past Birchington, Westgate, and Margate towards Longnose Buoy which marked the point at which we could begin to swing south to round the North Foreland. The log at this point has the following entry.

16.30 Longnose buoy abeam. Glass falling fairly rapidly. *Grayling* going like a bomb.

As we were going to be sailing into the eye of the wind as soon as we got round the corner and headed south, we kept on our easterly course for another half hour after passing Longnose, and made an offing of between 2 and 3 miles. *Grayling* was beginning to enjoy herself, but unfortunately Brian was not. There is always a bit of a popple off the Foreland, and though we had sailed round it together many times it often proved to be Brian's downfall. He never complained though, and ultimately conquered it. On one trip I gave him a seasickness pill and this did the trick. On the next trip I gave him a pill again, and it was particularly rough as we went round. When we were in smoother water he came up to me with the glint of triumph in his eye. He held out his hand, and in the palm was the pill, which he had kept in his pocket! That's the sort of shipmate to have!

But on this occasion he succumbed, and as we tacked down the coast in a wind that was obviously approaching gale force he must have suffered, but stuck to his job. After two longish boards we were in a position to fetch Ramsgate harbour, turned on to the port tack, and went creaming in towards the land. Here I made the mistake of not getting the mainsail off her before turning north to head for the harbour entrance. We were now on a dead run and travelling like an express train. Brian tried to get the mainsail down but it was beyond him. Bravely he took the tiller while I fought to get it down. We entered Ramsgate faster than I have ever been into any harbour before or since, and for a moment I thought we were going to go on up into the High Street!

To Brian's relief I took the tiller from him and managed to round up alongside the wall of the outer harbour, and we were both very grateful to be safe inside at last. As we straightened our backs after mooring up, Brian, remembering the man in the bowler hat who had accosted us in Queenborough earlier in the day, looked at me and said:

'Ramsgate?'

And only then did he collapse into his bunk.

There was still plenty to be done. The gates into the inner harbour were due to be opened at 21.00 and it was now 18.30, so I made arrangements for us to go in when they were opened, for it would be very much quieter inside, away from the big swell that was coming in through the entrance. But alas when the time came it was too rough for the gates to be opened and in the event I had a sleepless night adjusting fenders and warps as we ranged up and down the harbour wall. At midnight at the height of the storm continuous spray and occasional large dollops of solid water were coming over the wall, and it was very unpleasant.

At 02.15 the wind shifted into the south-west, which made life a little easier aboard, in that we were now being pressed against the wall all the time instead of being banged against it. This was harder on the fenders, but easier on the boat. But the gale blew all next day and it was still too rough to open the inner harbour gates. The Boulogne fishing fleet came in for shelter, and I think they were pretty glad to be in too.

Fortunately the little cafe on the pier kept open through it all and served plain but splendid hot meals, so we fared well. *Grayling* suffered no harm, and in fact gave us tremendous confidence in her abilities, for in an exciting and exhilarating sail she had demonstrated that she could cope with rough weather. In future storms I never had the slightest qualms about her seaworthiness — but we both always remembered our first sail in her to Ramsgate. On the morning after we arrived I was stopped by a man on the quay.

'Was it you who came in during the storm?' he asked.

I admitted that it was.

'A marvellous bit of seamanship if I may say so, sir!' he said. 'It was good to see a boat handled like that.'

If only he had known the near panic that reigned aboard!

10

Abroad to Calais and Ostend

A FEW days before we start our annual cruise the Met Office invariably forecast some strange weather in the offing — either gales, or flat calms, or rain, or fog — and very often we seem to get a mixture of the lot, and only occasionally a few hot sunny days with a good force 3 to 4 sailing breeze. But whatever the weather they throw at us it has absolutely no effect on the spirits of the crew, who have learned to improvize and make the best of anything that comes along. And this of course is the basis of a happy and healthy holiday.

We had all been looking forward for some time to our first annual holiday in *Grayling*, and it looked as though we were going to have a full crew. Sally was bringing her schoolfriend Jackie, Pat was coming, as were Geoff, Monk and Brian, and for the first part of the trip a new friend, Tom Aldis. Anthony, of course, was not able to be with us as he was already the mate of a working Thames sailing barge.

Tom was a little older than most of us, and had been a professional sailor all his life. During World War 2 he had been Master of two ships that had been torpedoed, and had had a terrible time. But he recovered

from his injuries, and after the war was made Master of the General Steam Navigation's new ship *Queen of the Channel*, which was based in the Thames and Medway. Unfortunately, she had an accident one night and went ashore on the French coast, and Tom was blamed for this. As a result his command was taken away from him and he subsequently left the company, and held no further position of command. Tom did not often sail with us, but when he did I liked to put him in charge of *Grayling*, for although she was a poor substitute for the *Queen of the Channel* she was at least his while he was aboard. On this trip he was only coming as far as Ramsgate.

The day our holiday started there was not a breath of wind. Not a breath. It was a perfect July day with a blue sky and hot sun, and as we did not intend to get under way until the evening the final preparations were unhurried and relaxed, and we had plenty of time to settle in. In the cool of the evening we dropped down the river on the engine and came to an anchor for the night in Stangate Creek, in near perfect conditions. Geoff and Monk were duty cooks, and prepared a super meal.

The following morning we were up early, and it looked like being another good day. It happened to be my birthday, and after breakfast I was serenaded by the crew and presented with a sock full of presents, including a sixpence, a lolly, a toffee apple, a rubber teapot spout, a baby's dummy, a torch battery, a stick of liquorice, a stick of barley sugar, a packet of sweet 'tobacco', an apple, a thermometer, a flash lamp bulb, a packet of envelopes, a comb, an orange, a small tin of Andrews Liver Salts, and a couple of egg cups. I suspected Geoff of being the instigator, though the others were, no doubt, willing accessories, and came to the conclusion that it was better not to try and read any message into some of the items.

We viewed the weather with mixed feelings. The sky was blue without a cloud in sight, and there was no wind. Ideal for some pursuits, such as sunbathing, but no good for sailing. Fortunately, the feminine members of the crew were all interested in sunbathing so there was no real problem, and the rest of us found plenty to do in the way of odd jobs. In the event it turned out to be a lazy but most pleasant day, and in the evening, when the heat had gone out of the sun, we motored round to Queenborough so that we would be ready for off very early in the morning. From the look of the sky it was apparent that we were in for a weather change, and the late forecast predicted westerly winds, force 6.

The following day the log opens with the words:

04.35 Up early, but not bright.

The wind was blowing about force 4 but the sky was cloudy and troubled, and the prospects of having a fast sail with plenty of wind were good.

By 06.00 we were ready to go, High Water Sheerness being at 06.58. Force 4 was a good breeze for *Grayling* and she slipped through the water majestically with the wind on her port quarter, and we were soon running down the buoyed big ship channel out of the Medway. At buoy No 8 we turned to cross the Cant and headed for the Spile buoy. The ebb was beginning to run and with a following wind *Grayling* fairly galloped along. The Spile was abeam at 08.00, exactly one hour after leaving Garrison Point, giving us a speed over the ground of about 7 knots, of which 1 knot was perhaps due to the tide. Time for our second breakfast, the first one having been a rather sketchy affair at 05.00 when we were hardly awake.

From the Spile to the West Last is about 10½ miles and we covered this in an hour and a half, showing that our speed over the ground was being maintained. It was a smooth but exhilarating ride, the sea being comparatively calm, and *Grayling* surged along. After I had entered up this information in the log I looked back at the figures recorded some weeks before when Brian and I had made the same trip, and was interested to see that today we had covered the eighteen miles from Sheerness twenty minutes quicker. Maybe we had a little more tide under us, and the wind was a touch stronger.

The next leg, to Longnose, was about nine miles and was equally fast. Here we were on a dead run, with the boom squared off, and at least some of the time with the jib goose-winged. The wind was freshening all the time and we were soon round the corner and heading south. I reckoned the wind was a good force 5 gusting to 6, and quite a big following sea had built up with many whitecaps. On the starboard tack, with sheets hauled in, *Grayling* heeled over and was off like a greyhound, a bone between her teeth.

And then it happened. Without any warning, in one of the gusts, both starboard main shrouds parted with a noise like a pistol shot. The mast, which was a solid spruce spar, bent like a bow, and for a moment or two I thought we were going to lose it. It was an instinctive reaction to put her about on to the port tack so that the weight of wind in the sails was taken by the port shrouds, and the problem then was to get the mainsail off her as soon as possible, for we were now heading straight for the cliffs near Broadstairs at a considerable rate of knots. The cliffs were probably about a mile away but seemed much nearer at the speed we were doing, but once the sails were off we slowed right down and just wallowed in the sea.

Panic subsided, the engine was started, and we proceeded sedately on our way, all the excitement and exhilaration having been suddenly lost. We set a small spitfire jib, but even this bent the mast in the most frightening way, so we limped on into Ramsgate without any sail at all. Personally I was in a very thoughtful frame of mind, for I had never seen a solid spar bend like that without breaking. It was very alarming. Examination of the broken shrouds showed that the shackles that had attached them to the band round the mast at the hounds had pulled out, and we consoled ourselves with the knowledge that we were not far from Ramsgate where we should be able to get a professional repair job done quickly.

How wrong we were! I will refrain from mentioning the name of the boatyard, for the rigger they sent aboard began by saying the mast would have to come out. I persuaded him that this was surely unnecessary, and he came back later with two colleagues and a long ladder, and then for the next six days their riggers Sidney and George were on and off the boat at all times — with and without ladders — while we fretted and fumed. The problem was that they felt they had to make up a new mast band with lugs welded on, and they had to send out to have this done.

At last it was finished and we were able to continue our cruise, though I must confess that while we were stuck in Ramsgate there had been gale warnings every day and we would not have been able to go very far anyway. Also we had quite enjoyed ourselves in harbour, and had taken the opportunity of overhauling one of the sea cocks that was weeping, and of putting *Grayling* alongside the wall and giving her bottom a badly needed scrub. But it was with joyful hearts that we set sail for Dover in a force 3 sou-westerly breeze which was steadily freshening.

Three hours later, when we were still a few miles short of Dover, the starboard main shrouds parted again. To say that this was disappointing is to put it very mildly indeed for the wind was certainly no more than force 4 at the time, and the repair carried out in Ramsgate had been not only lengthy but also expensive. There was nothing for it but to start the engine once again and plod on to Dover. Fortunately the engine started easily and ran without complaint, though we all kept our fingers crossed for we had been having trouble through dirt in the petrol. Perhaps the presence of Monk in the crew influenced the engine: he was a great engineer and the engine knew this and realized who was the boss.

In Dover we dropped anchor in the Submarine Basin on the east side of the harbour. Today this would have been impossible for Dover is now so busy as a ferry port that yachtsmen are not really welcome, and certainly have to keep to the western end of the harbour, well away from the main commercial activity. But thirty years ago the Submarine Basin — so called because of some First World War submarine pens — was a quiet and peaceful haven where there was always plenty of water, easy access to the shore, and where the white cliffs towered over the anchorage. The cries of the seagulls echoed from the cliffs and gave this part of the harbour a fascinating character all of its own and always made it a pleasure to visit.

By the time sails were stowed and sheets neatly coiled — and with such a large and willing crew this did not take long — I had decided what to do about the shrouds, and was kicking myself for not having done it in Ramsgate. There was a small boatyard on the quay and next morning I got them to make up for me some wire strops with thimbles spliced in at each end. Each strop was the right length to go round the mast at the hounds so that the two thimbles came together and could be shackled to a shroud. This may not sound a very elegant solution, but it worked, and we had no more trouble.

While we were doing this the weather produced another series of gales and thunderstorms but we were far from bored. Indeed, in spite of the adverse weather conditions and the shroud troubles the holiday was turning out to be most enjoyable. There was another yacht in the Submarine Basin, *Melisande*, the owner of which Pat knew. He was in fact her dentist in London, but we decided not to hold this against him for it was not necessarily his fault. Not that I wish to say anything disparaging about dentistry, which is an honourable and necessary profession, but I was put off dentists when I was a teenager and living in Yorkshire. My dentist was a remarkable man who had originally been a miner at the coal face. He had studied in his spare time to begin with and had ultimately qualified. In practice he turned out to be brilliant, but was to my mind rather heavy handed. He was known locally, to all and sundry as 'Jack the Ripper'.

During the next few stormy days we saw a lot of Ken and Joyce from *Melisande* and enjoyed their company. Joyce was an organizer, and keen on fishing, and before we knew where we were she had us all out on the breakwater fishing. We did not catch anything of course but it was a new experience to many of us. Later we caught two pollock in the Submarine Basin, but foolishly left these on deck while we went ashore, and the seagulls had them. Joyce caught an eel and cooked it in her pressure cooker, and though some of us had misgivings about eating it, it was in fact delicious.

The next day she had us out on a picnic in Lyminge forest where we played rounders until we were exhausted, and staggered back to the boat to recuperate. Fortunately the weather then moderated and we were able to get back to the object of the holiday, which was sailing. If the bad weather had persisted I shudder to think what Joyce would have had us doing next.

We left the Submarine Basin at 09.30 the following morning for Calais, the sky being overcast with low cloud and mist, and visibility poor. The wind was easterly force 3 and the sea was slight, but the prospect was of more wind and sea to come. High Water Dover was at 13.05.

The navigation from Dover to Calais is pretty simple, the distance being only about 22 miles, but in a slow speed sailing boat you have to think very carefully about tidal streams which are strong and which run athwart your course, carrying you either one way or the other. So that providing you can estimate the speed of your ship in the conditions that obtain, you can make due allowance for the set of the tide and steer a course which will bring you to the entrance to Calais harbour, though the bow of your ship may not actually be pointing at it until you arrive.

That is the theory, but on this occasion I got it wrong, allowed too much for westward drift, and by the time we saw the French coast — only about a mile away in the poor visibility — I was shocked to find we were well to the west of Calais. This in itself was no great problem for the tide turned to the east at high water and so was helping us along, but the wind had increased to between 5 and 6 and was heading us, so that we had to tack. The sea also became rough, and for the last hour and a half we had a pretty bumpy ride and took a lot of spray aboard, from which on *Grayling*'s flush deck there was no shelter. The log says:

> 14.15 Entered Calais, sea confused in entrance, and *Grayling* difficult to steer. Engine refused to start when needed. Big swell in the harbour.

The log discreetly says little about the Skipper's poor navigation, but it does point out, rather smugly, that the repair to the starboard shrouds appeared to be perfectly OK.

Calais is not the most glamorous of French cities but the old town is interesting, and of course the harbour dominated by its huge lighthouse is fascinating. We have always had rather a fond feeling for Calais, possibly because it was for many years an English town, and was in fact the last of our European possessions to be lost. As previously reported we lived — when the children were small — in the Old Customs House in Sandwich, a house in which Queen Philippa, wife of King Edward III, is reputed to have stayed while awaiting a fair wind for France. She was on her way to join the King at Calais where he had just raised the seige, and where she was subsequently to plead with her husband to spare the lives of the six burghers who offered themselves as a sacrifice if only he would spare the town. I still remember one of my first stage appearances as a very small boy at Prep School playing the part (non-speaking) of one of these burghers.

Calais was lost in 1558 and Queen Mary Tudor who died shortly afterwards said that the word 'Calais' would be found engraved on her heart. But on this day we had no such sombre thoughts, the sun came out, it was warm and pleasant, and for two days we behaved like the tourists we were. The girls spent much of their time on the beach which is wide and sandy, and is backed by extensive dunes. The men stayed nearer home, doing the odd job on the boat, exploring the town, and buying the necessary provisions for a picnic lunch.

One of the most enjoyable things about visiting France is the snack lunch of bread, butter, cheese and wine. Why doesn't English bread ever taste like French bread, nor English butter like French butter? It must be because French bread is freshly baked and contains no preservative, whereas in England the bread so often has the appearance and consistency of sponge rubber and has had, by some clever chemical process, its taste entirely removed. The same criticism can be levelled at the butter, for even the unsalted butter in England does not taste as good as the French variety. And when you add to French bread and butter some of the delicious cheeses which are obtainable anywhere in France, and which are so different to the soap-like mousetrap stuff we are offered in England, and wash it all down with a glass of red wine, you have a snack lunch fit for a king.

Perhaps the wine is the biggest puzzle of all, for in any food shop in France you can buy a bottle of red wine, often unlabelled, and costing only a few francs, which will be better quality than many brands in this country costing ten times the price. We are told that this cheap French 'plonk' will not travel, this being the reason why we don't see it in this country, but there must be more to it than that. After all it travels the full length of France satisfactorily. Perhaps by the time it has been given a gaudy label, and has passed through several hands, it reaches the consumer in England as a chateau-bottled product at a price the ordinary man cannot afford.

After two days of laziness we felt we ought to be on our way again, and decided to visit Dunkirk.

12.10	Dropped moorings and proceeded out of the Bassin Carnot under engine. Set sail in outer harbour, and so to sea.
12.30	Pierheads abeam. Wind light westerly, sea slight, visibility good. H.W.13.26. Tide already setting strongly to eastward, so a 'downhill' sail to Dunkirk. Turned to starboard, freed the sheets, and squared off the boom.
14.15	Gravelines entrance abeam, distant about 2 miles.
16.35	Entered Dunkirk. Started engine, handed sails.
17.30	After a trip up the harbour into shallow water finally tied up alongside *Roxanne*, a yacht we had last seen in Dover.

The following wind and eastward running tide had given us a very pleasant, lazy sail in hot sunshine. The following day we were off again, having paid our respects to Dunkirk. Although this visit was made ten years after the war was over, and fifteen since the evacuation of the British Army, there was still an atmosphere about the place. Our feelings were very mixed, being compounded of pride in the magnificent work done by the Royal Navy and the flotilla of other ships, humility in that this should ever have been necessary, and great sadness at the tragic and senseless waste of human life. There were several wrecks still lying off the beach, and I guess it will be a long time before the spirit of the place recovers. We could not wait to get away from it.

Having cleared the pierheads we found a bit of a popple outside and a westerly breeze of about force 4. Heading up into the wind, while Monk anxiously watched the engine, Geoff went up forward to hoist the jib, and I can still see him holding on for dear life while *Grayling* almost stood up on end as she climbed over a particularly short steep wave. As soon as the sails were set we turned to the eastwards and shut down the engine, and once we had made an offing of about a mile the sea quietened down. For the next four hours we had a glorious downwind sail and romped along, the only incident being when Geoff, who was on the tiller, went rather too close to an enormous pillar buoy in Ostend Roads. He had not realized just how big this brute was, and when it rolled towards us I thought for a moment we were going to hit it. The log records that at 16.45 we turned to enter Ostend, and that by 17.10 we were safely and snugly moored outside the North Sea Yacht Club.

We decided to stay in Ostend for two or three days before turning for home for we were now beginning to run out of time and wanted to savour the delights of this very popular resort, as well as enjoy the hospitality of the North Sea Yacht Club. After we had tidied up the ship — we liked to have the neatest stow of any yacht in the harbour — we tidied ourselves and sallied ashore for something to eat. There are many superb little restaurants in the streets near the harbour and there is never any problem in getting a good meal at reasonable cost.

After we left the restaurant we walked along the street and soon passed a building from which the noise of human voices, music and laughter was coming. It looked like a cafe, but the curtains were tightly drawn, and the doorway was dark and slightly mysterious. However we could make out the name of the establishment — it was 'Chez Van' — so wondering what we were in for we pushed open the door and went in. The inside was not really mysterious at all, just a medium-sized room full of people enjoying themselves, drinking, talking, and laughing. The lights were dimmish but kept changing, and the atmosphere was noisy and friendly.

At the far side of the room was a bar, and at one end of the bar sat the proprietor, Monsieur Van, watching the scene before him and controlling the lights from a small switchboard. He spoke very good English and appeared pleased to see us, and we soon felt quite at home. He accepted the drink we offered him and chatted away to us in the most friendly fashion imaginable.

Now, Monk was a great collector of ashtrays, and he thought an ashtray from 'Chez Van' would be a suitable addition to *Grayling*'s saloon, so he asked Van if he could let us have one. Van responded with alacrity and caused one of his barmen to bring us no less than three, and from then on the *entente* became even more *cordiale*, and in short we spent a thoroughly pleasant hour or so with him. When it was time to go he asked if we were staying in Ostend, and queried whether we had any beer mats on our boat. When we told him we had not, he said 'Come back tomorrow night, and I will have some beer mats for you!' With that we shook hands all round, said good-bye, and staggered back to *Grayling* clutching our ashtrays.

It occurred to us that such generosity as he had displayed ought to be rewarded, and we discussed the possibility of a suitable gift. On the walls of his bar we had noticed one or two yacht club burgees pinned up, so thought it might be a good idea to give him one of ours, and back on the boat I went through our flags and found two which we could manage without. So next night we turned up as before and duly presented Monsieur Van with the burgees of two English yacht clubs.

He was absolutely delighted with these and (metaphorically) offered us the top brick off his chimney. He dived under the bar and produced a whole carton of beer mats which he thrust into our slightly embarrassed hands. This called for drinks all round, and after we had pledged each other's health, he excused himself for a moment and came back with two further cartons, each of which contained a dozen lager glasses. By the time we left we had got over our embarrassment and were firm friends of his. His parting remark to us was:

'Come back next year — and bring a lorry!'

After this bout of euphoria we were naturally even more reluctant to leave Ostend, but some of us had to get back to work, and indeed Monk was so pressed for time that he caught the ferry the following morning and was in London by the time we had reached Dover.

Our voyage back to England was pleasant, relaxing, and reasonably speedy, taking exactly ten hours for a distance of about sixty miles. There was only one incident on the way. There had been some news of stray World War 2 mines having been seen in the southern North Sea, and yachtsmen had been advised to use the swept channel between Ostend and Dunkirk. This we did, but off Nieuport we were approached at high speed by a Belgian Air Force launch. He made no attempt to communicate with us but passed close enough to create a wash that sent things sliding about in the cockpit. We took a photograph of him as he swooped past, uttered a few rude words, and then forgot about it. But when the photograph was developed we saw he had been flying the International Signal Flag 'U', which means 'You are standing into danger!'

11

The lighter side

WITH *Grayling*'s draught of 6 ft 9 in it was easy to go aground — very easy. In the Medway area, and particularly in some of the creeks, there was more mud than water at low tide and it was difficult to remember that *Grayling* could not be taken into many places where shoal draught yachts were able to sail with impunity. All things considered we did not go aground very often, but inevitably there were occasions when we slipped up and found we had come to a halt, with the dinghy catching us up and bumping *Grayling*'s counter stern to remind us.

When this happened on a rising tide and in reasonable weather it was not a serious matter. All you had to do was to sit there patiently and wait for the tide to lift you off, although it was not always easy to be patient in these circumstances, especially if there were other yachts about, perhaps passing you and smiling condescendingly. Various people did tell me that it was possible to be trapped so firmly in soft mud that the tide would not have the power to free the boat, and that ultimately the water level would rise until it came over the gunwale and sank the yacht, but I am happy to say that this gruesome fate was spared us.

But if you went aground on a falling tide this could be much more serious. I never actually saw *Grayling* lying down on her side, but from her hull shape I think the angle would have been horrific, and there might have been a real danger of her filling when the tide came back. So it was a matter of some importance to prevent this from happening.

How we came to develop the technique for keeping her upright when she was on the mud and the tide was falling I do not now remember, but develop it — and perfect it — we did, and I can remember a couple of occasions when it served us in very good stead. One of these was in Brightlingsea in Essex, the entrance of which is a little on the shallow side for *Grayling*, although it was in fact her birthplace. But the other was in Queenborough in the River Swale, just off the River Medway.

For many years Queenborough had a sort of short pier, built for the use of passenger steamers, and there was deepish water reasonably close to this, but this pier was derelict for a long time and the day came when the decision was taken to demolish it. The difference this made to the scenery as you came sweeping into Queenborough was not very great, but it meant that the deep water channel was further from the shore than it had been from the end of the pier and you had to be careful.

The first time we came in after the demolition we were on the engine, and Brian happened to be on the tiller. We were travelling at a fair old lick, and he kept too far over to port, not realizing that the pier was no longer there, with the result that he went charging up the mud. There appeared to be lots of water all around but she was stuck fast and the ebb was beginning to flow. Going astern on the engine was tried, as was the trick of trying to rock the boat from side to side, but neither was to any avail.

The drill designed for just such a situation was then put into operation, and it was performed so quickly and efficiently that within minutes the necessary steps had been taken to ensure that *Grayling* did not fall over when the tide left her. This drill did in fact cause hilarity amongst some people, and perhaps it did look a little odd, but it was very simple and very effective. The first step was to detach the main halyard from the mainsail and attach it to the bower anchor, which was then taken off in the dinghy broad on the starboard side. It was taken as far as possible before being let go. While this was being done the jib halyard was being bent on to the kedge, and as soon as the dinghy returned from laying out the bower anchor it took out the kedge on the port side and again laid it out as far from the boat as possible.

That was all that was necessary, and we found from experience that *Grayling* was quite stable — assuming that the mud was reasonably soft and her keel had dug in a bit — and it was possible to move about fairly freely aboard even when she was high and dry. There was in fact a very useful bonus, in that the crew could utilize some of the waiting hours by giving the bottom a scrub at low water, the helmsman who was responsible for the incident naturally being made to play a major part in this chore. It took Brian some time to live this one down, but it could have happened to any of us.

With Brian, Geoff, and Monk aboard there were not many dull moments, and at times life was positively hilarious, for they all had a sense of humour and were prone to practical jokes. Some of this humour was perhaps schoolboyish, but at the time it was very funny, and helped to create and preserve a fantastic spirit amongst the crew. I remember one night when we went to bed very late and had to be up early so that we were anxious to get to sleep, but even this did not prevent a bout of horseplay breaking out.

The girls were sleeping in the bunks aft, and the four men were in the saloon, two on the settee berths and two on the cabin sole. We each had a sleeping bag, a blanket, and a cushion, and as luck would have it there was a cushion left over that no one wanted. After the light was put out and we had all said goodnight I was just settling down peacefully when the spare cushion landed on me. Well, naturally I had to dispose of it, and threw it across to the other berth. From there it went to someone on the floor, and in no time at all the air seemed to be full of cushions and blankets. Ultimately, we were all so thoroughly awake that we got up and made a pot of tea!

Sally was in her teens at this time and was a great favourite with the rest of the crew. She was perpetually having her leg pulled over the frequency with which she went to the loo, and Geoff, Monk, and Brian soon christened it 'Sally's Saloon'. Ultimately they had a smart brass plate made up, which Brian took to work one day and had engraved with just these words: on our next trip they brought it with them and screwed it on to the loo door while one of them kept Sally occupied ashore.

This incident reminded me of the occasion when we took the children to Paris, having just made our first channel crossing in *Merlin*. Sally was very small at the time and we were out sightseeing one afternoon when she decided she wanted to spend a penny. We were passing the Surete, the French Scotland Yard at this moment, a very imposing building, and I asked the gendarme on the gate where the nearest public toilet was. This flummoxed him, but he invited us to enter the building where he said we should be sure to find one somewhere. So we spent a few amazing minutes wandering around, up and down corridors, with no one taking any notice of us, and finally stopped a woman carrying a sheaf of papers, and she directed us up on to the fourth floor, where we found what we wanted.

We were lucky in *Grayling* in that Geoff, Monk, and Brian were all excellent cooks and did not mind sharing this work. The log has frequent references to the fact that they dished up a superb meal on this or that occasion, and in this and many other respects the ship had a very contented skipper.

Geoff was perhaps the most imaginative of the three chefs, and you never knew what he would produce next. Round about this time the first instant potato came on the market. This was called 'Pom', and Geoff was very taken with its possibilities, particularly with the claim that even chips could be fabricated from it. One afternoon as we were on our way back to the Medway from Dover, and were crossing the Cant, Geoff retired below, without telling anyone, to experiment, and we had no idea what he was up to until he appeared on deck with a yachting cap on back to front, a napkin over his arm, and carrying a plate of chips.

Solemnly he handed them round, to appreciative remarks from the crew, saving the last one for me. He stood beside me as I ate it, balancing the empty plate on the fingers of one hand, and then, without a flicker of an eyelid, as soon as I had approved his skill, he tossed the plate nonchalantly over his shoulder into the sea. Naturally I looked surprised, for it was one of our best plates, and then he laughed. He said afterwards that the look on my face was worth more than the cost of six plates.

From her earliest days as a sailor Sally had always made herself responsible for the flags aboard the boat, and for flag etiquette. In those days there were not so many yachts about, and we still observed the old customs and traditions such as taking down the burgee at sunset, whenever possible taking our time from the most senior yacht in the harbour, and of flying the ship's 'number' as a means of identification when leaving or entering port, and I was very pleased that my daughter became a stickler for observing these practices. *Grayling*'s number consisted of the signal letters MDYY, and we carried the four flags made up in a hoist. When we came into port Sally would always see that our number was flying from the crosstrees, so that the port authorities knew who we were.

Coming into Sheerness one day she hoisted the number and soon afterwards a Customs launch came out to intercept us. The officer in charge hailed us through a megaphone, saying:

'What ship are you?'

I was just about to reply when Sally said 'No, Dad!' and pointed to the number above her. He hailed us again but she would not let anyone answer, and ultimately he got the message and went below to look up the owner of MDYY, but Sally was not always the cause of such embarrassment.

Indeed, I remember one occasion in Ramsgate when I had to leave the boat unexpectedly and go up to London for a couple of days. At this time we were flying the Little Ship Club burgee and wearing the Club's defaced blue ensign, for which privilege I had an Admiralty warrant. Now, this warrant was granted to me personally, and the stipulation was that the blue ensign to which it referred was not to be worn unless I was aboard and in charge of the boat. On this occasion I said goodbye to them all and climbed up on to the quay, turning at the top to take one last look at *Grayling*. As I looked, Sally was at the ensign staff, taking down the blue and replacing it with the red ensign.

Silly? Perhaps, but it did me good to know that the rules and the old traditions were being observed in my own little ship.

12

Maylandsea mooring and the Blackwater

IN A previous chapter I remarked on the rapidity with which the weather can change in this country, how one day it can be warm, sunny, and apparently settled, and yet within 24 hours the bottom can fall out of the barometer and we have to contend with cold winds and rain, and all sorts of nastiness.

And so with life — or at any rate with my life — for changes came along, suddenly and with relentless rapidity, changes for which I was quite unprepared and with which I was unable to cope, so that I was left baffled, bewildered, and lost. Up to this point my domestic life and career had both been apparently successful and settled. I had been married for sixteen years and had two marvellous children of whom I was very proud; prospects for promotion in my job were excellent: the barometer seemed to be set fair. And yet within a year all this had changed. Our houseboat *Magnet* was sold, my marriage came to an end, and in the confusion and disillusion that followed I resigned my job, and went from one foolishness to another. Only *Grayling* and her crew, and my friends, remained constant.

But before actually leaving Rochester to live in Harlow New Town,

where my new job was, we had one final sailing season in the Medway and I found a mooring for *Grayling* further down the river at the Medway Cruising Club in Gillingham. This mooring was never very satisfactory and I lived in perpetual fear of receiving a message that *Grayling* had dragged it, and herself, out into the main channel leading to the entrance to Chatham Dockyard which was nearby. This she did more than once and the Queen's Harbour Master was not amused.

The trouble was probably due to the poor nature of the holding ground on the bed of the river, to the fairly fierce tides, and also possibly the fact that the mooring was too light, although it consisted of two enormous anchors separated by a long length of very heavy chain. But *Grayling* was a very strong and wilful young lady, there was lots of her under the water, and she seemed to have no difficulty at all in rolling the whole mooring up into a great jangled ball of chain, anchors and mud, which she then lifted as the tide rose and carried with her wheresoever she wanted to go.

Towards the end of that season we decided to sail over to Brightlingsea to attend the Little Ship Club end of season rally. Though we were none of us dedicated rallyers we knew we would meet many old friends there, and make new ones, and Brightlingsea had long been a favourite port of call. We were a strangely depleted crew — Pat, Geoff, Monk and myself — but at least we each had a bunk to sleep in, and we went aboard on the Friday evening, the idea being to drop down the river and anchor off Deadman Island below Stangate, so that we could make an early start in the morning.

In the event, as so often happens, it worked out differently, and we did not drop our anchor until half an hour after midnight. And then of course we sat and talked until 4.00 am although for part of this time Monk and Geoff tinkered with the engine and dismantled the clutch, which had been slipping. After about 2½ hours sleep I turned out to prepare for off, only to find thick fog, so I decided to wait until it cleared a bit — crossing the Thames estuary in fog is always a bit dicey.

We were away soon after 8 o'clock in a flat calm and no wind, but with a nice ebb tide. We cleared the Garrison by 08.45 and two hours later had safely crossed the shipping lanes without getting run down and were heading down Swin. At 14.40 we entered the Spitway between the Buxey and Gunfleet Sands, and at 15.00 precisely the Wallet Spitway Buoy was abeam. From then on it was a fairly straightforward sail into the River Colne and we arrived in Brightlingsea at 16.30.

We spent a thoroughly enjoyable evening in the Colne Yacht Club at the rally, almost the first old friend I met being Stanley Swan who had

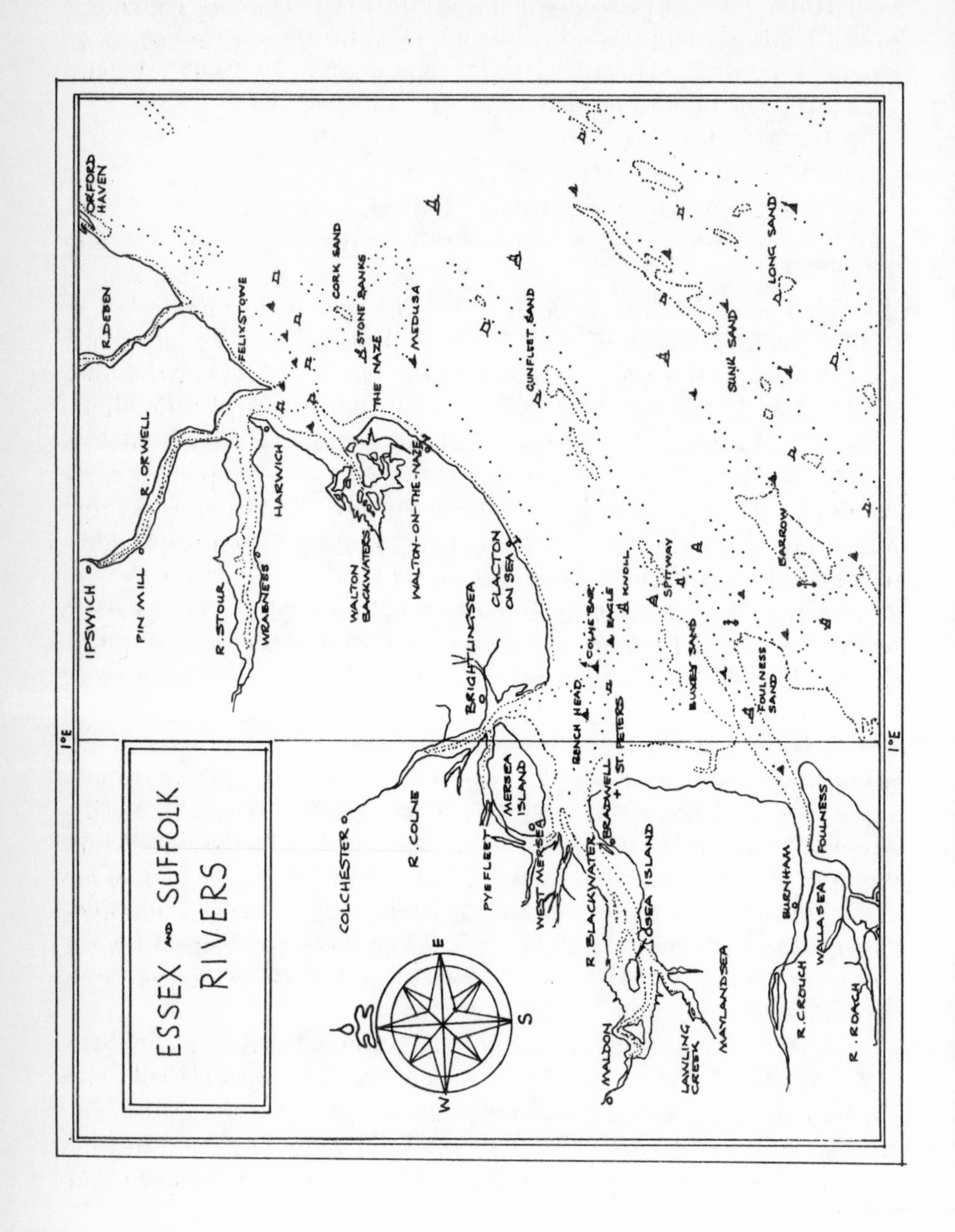
ESSEX AND SUFFOLK
RIVERS
IPSWICH
PIN MILL
R. ORWELL
R. DEBEN
ORFORD HAVEN
FELIXSTOWE
R. STOUR
WRABNESS
HARWICH
CORK SAND
STONE BANKS
THE NAZE
MEDUSA
WALTON BACKWATERS
WALTON-ON-THE-NAZE
CLACTON ON SEA
GUNFLEET SAND
BRIGHTLINGSEA
COLCHESTER
R. COLNE
MERSEA ISLAND
PYEFLEET
WEST MERSEA
BENCH HEAD
COLNE BAR
EAGLE
KNOLL
SPITWAY
BUXEY SAND
ST. PETERS
BRADWELL
R. BLACKWATER
OSEA ISLAND
MALDON
LAWLING CREEK
MAYLANDSEA
SUNK SAND
LONG SAND
BARROW
FOULNESS SAND
BURNHAM
FOULNESS
WALLASEA
R. CROUCH
R. ROACH
1°E
1°E
W
E
S

helped me to sail *Merlin* from Gosport to Sandwich. Another friend was Fred Armes, the local photographer whose picture of *Grayling* is included in this book. He had taken this picture from his little speedboat as we entered Brightlingsea to attend the previous year's Little Ship Club Rally. Fred introduced me to his wife, saying:

'Darling, this is Mr Winter.'

'Oh yes' she said, 'Mr C.W.R. Winter.'

'How do you know my initials?' I asked.

'Oh!' she said brightly, 'We always refer to you as Cold, Wet, and Rainy!'

That year the weather held until the end of October when it suddenly turned very cold, and our last weekend afloat was a very gentle affair, although this was partly due to the fact that I was busy with a production of Noel Coward's *Hay Fever* at the delightful little Globe Theatre in Chatham Dockyard. In rehearsal this play went smoothly enough until the day of the dress rehearsal when the girl playing Myra Arundel, the vamp, was ordered to bed by her doctor. We were lucky that Jeanne Lee, one of the Society's most talented members, who came down to the theatre to help backstage, took on the part without turning a hair, and made a huge success of it. Besides being of stout heart Jeanne was a really accomplished actress, and on the opening night she sailed through the part without a single prompt, and she did this in spite of an incident in Act II which would have thrown a lesser mortal.

In this Act Myra has a little scene with David, the father of the family whose house she is visiting, and David (the part I was playing) has to make a pass at her as they sit side by side on a settee. Jeanne was wearing dingle-dangle earrings and a dress with a low cut back, and as she resisted David's advances one of the earrings came off and dropped down the back of her dress. Fortunately it did not go too far, and having my arm round her I managed to retrieve it. The desire to laugh was very strong and I saw the corners of her mouth twitch, but that was all and her concentration never faltered — marvellous!

After the last performance on the Saturday night Monk, Geoff, Sally and I rejoined *Grayling* and the following day had a leisurely sail down the river and back, which was a very pleasant way to end the season. Two weeks later Pat and I took *Grayling* into Gillingham Dock and had her mast lifted out, following which Monk and Geoff joined us and we took her upstream to Borstal where we laid her up for the winter.

This turned out to be the last time that *Grayling* was laid up in the Medway area, for when the next season came along I was searching for a suitable mooring for her in Essex. We had already visited the Essex Rivers

Colne, Crouch, Roach and Blackwater more than once, and had enjoyed them, so that the opportunity to go and live amongst them was quite an exciting prospect, and it alleviated to a large extent the sadness we felt at leaving Kent which had given us many happy hours of sailing and was such a convenient stepping off point for the continent.

The mooring I found was at Maylandsea in Lawling Creek, an offshoot of the Blackwater, and very satisfactory it turned out to be, its only snag being a long row from the boatyard at the head of the creek. But this was a minor disadvantage, and Maylandsea turned out to be an excellent centre for exploring the Essex and Suffolk coastline. How we came to take possession of our new mooring was in this wise.

In my new job at Harlow I found a friend in Tommy Ash, who was chief engineer of the small company of which I was works manager. Tommy had a sailing boat which he kept in Maylandsea, and it was he who pointed me in that direction when looking for a mooring. So it was arranged that when we arrived in *Grayling* he and his children would be around in *April* to welcome us. On this occasion *Grayling*'s crew was small but select, and comprised Anthony, Pat, and another friend of ours, John Oliver. Anthony by this time was eighteen and was waiting to be called up for National Service. He had given up his sailing barge job and, pending his call-up, was working for an old friend of ours, Captain O.M. Watts, the yacht chandler of Albemarle Street, for whom Pat also worked.

John Oliver was, and still is, a friend of the family, and is a man that I feel privileged to call a friend, for John was born with the handicap of having no proper arms, and with one leg shorter than the other. I hesitate to use the word 'handicap', for what most of us would regard as a tremendous drawback John has transformed into a triumphant feature. He is more able-bodied than many men I know who possess a full set of normal arms and legs, and to see him on a boat is to be baffled and amazed. He could swig up *Grayling*'s mainsail as well as any of us, and he was equally proficient at delicate operations such as opening a packet of cigarettes, taking one out, and lighting it with a match, all of which was done with his feet.

There seemed to be no limit to what he could do, and over and over again I marvelled at his ability and dexterity. At this time I was a heavy pipe smoker, and one day when we were sailing together and *Grayling* was proving difficult to handle and causing me to struggle with the tiller, he said:

'Would you like me to fill your pipe, Skipper?'

Not everybody can fill a pipe satisfactorily, even when they have plenty of fingers and thumbs, and to be able to do it when you have no hands at all is frankly incredible, but John could do it, and do it perfectly, so that the pipe smoked smoothly and evenly all the way through. I could go on writing about his achievements, about how he bought his own work boat on the River Medway, and made a living with it, how he learned to drive a car and toured as far as Scotland. And particularly about his temperament and his friendly and cheerful disposition, for John Oliver is an example and inspiration to us all.

By the time we arrived in the Blackwater we were all slightly damp, for the weather was squally and blowing between force 5 and 6. *April* was on station at the entrance to Lawling Creek and escorted us to our new home. When we were safely moored and tidied up Tommy Ash and his children came aboard for tea and we had a very friendly get-together. I shall long remember the expressions of incredulity on the childrens' faces as John handed round the plate of sandwiches with his foot.

★ ★ ★

There were several reasons why we had looked forward eagerly to being domiciled in Essex. Firstly, it would enable us to renew acquaintance with many delightful anchorages we had visited both in *Merlin* and in *Grayling*, and also it gave us the opportunity of exploring a little further afield. The Essex and Suffolk rivers were very different from those of the north Kent coast, they had a character and a fascination all of their own, possibly because they were more remote and less frequented than their Kentish equivalents. The Medway and its many creeks provide excellent sailing, but you are never very far away from the three sprawling Medway towns, Rochester, Chatham, and Gillingham at one end, and Sheerness and the Isle of Grain oil refinery at the other. Nowadays there is also a power station in the lower reaches.

Essex has Colchester and Maldon, and Suffolk has Ipswich, but these are smaller, country towns situated well inland, and their influence is not felt in the estuaries. Here there are, or were, anchorages so lonely and peaceful that you could imagine yourselves hundreds of miles from civilization. Swatchways, the magic of which Maurice Griffiths wrote about, places like Paglesham on the River Roach, Pyefleet Creek behind Mersea Island, and the Walton Backwaters. In such places true peace and quiet is to be found, where the only sounds are the crying of the terns and curlews, the rustle of the wind on the marsh, and the sibilant susurration of the mud as it is uncovered by the ebbing tide.

The Essex coastline too, with its huge range of sands — Maplin,

Foulness, Buxey and Gunfleet — is full of interest and sailing history. There is always a thrill in sighting the Whitaker Beacon, that solitary sentinal over five miles from the nearest land, marking the beginning of the Whitaker Channel into the Crouch and Roach, and in the old days as you sailed down Swin it was a common sight to see a dozen or more sailing barges beating up against the wind for the London river. If you were bound for Burnham you rounded the Whitaker Beacon and hopped the buoys right into the River Crouch, but for Brightlingsea you held your course until the Swin Spitway buoy was found. Once through the Spitway into the Wallet the coastline of Colne rapidly unfolded before you and the choice of Colne or Blackwater was yours.

The Colne of course we already knew through having visited Brightlingsea several times, but the Blackwater was comparatively new to us. Apart from the one occasion when we had sailed up as far as Osea Island in *Merlin*, and where she had dragged her anchor and sunk, we had no knowledge of the river. But we soon found that the Blackwater was a most interesting river, full of attractions and equally full of dangers. At its mouth where it joins the Colne and both run into the sea, it is a mile and a half wide, a large expanse of water ideal for shoal draught craft, but its width is a snare and a delusion for the deep water channel is less than half a mile, and with *Grayling*'s draught it was very necessary to keep to this channel except at the top of the tide.

At the head of the navigable part of the river lies Maldon, a delightful little town which has been a boating and sailing barge centre for centuries, but at low water it dries out completely and you have to be prepared to take the ground. Fortunately the mud is very soft and many boats, especially Thames sailing barges, can sit upright in it, but it is of no use to yachts with a hull shape like *Grayling*.

About six miles below Maldon is the entrance to Lawling Creek, where we had our mooring, and opposite to Lawling Creek is Osea Island. This small island, which at low water is connected to the mainland by a rude causeway, always looked deserted and rather sinister, and this may have been due to the fact that for many years the only house in the island was a home for alcoholics.

Below Osea on the port hand lie some fascinating creeks and marshes — Goldhanger and Thirstlet, and the villages of Goldhanger, Tollesbury, Tolleshunt Major and Tolleshunt D'Arcy — all remote and all interesting. At Tollesbury many years ago a major development was attempted by bringing the railway to the village and building a pier, the desire being to establish a link with the continent and take some lucrative trade away from Harwich and Parkeston Quay. But this never caught on, and ultimately the pier was demolished, only the piles being left. The Tollesbury marshes are very wild, and railway traffic would have ruined them, so perhaps it was a blessing that this development failed. During the 1939-45 war the 10th Battalion the Essex Home Guard, of which I was a member, used the army rifle range on these marshes for practicing with live ammunition and learning how to throw grenades — another desecration of the solitude.

At the eastern end of the Tollesbury marshes are the villages of Salcott and Virley, lying at the head of the Salcott channel, one of the many branches of an intricate creek system which separates Mersea Island from the mainland. This area of the Blackwater is so full of interest and history that there is no wonder that it has become the busiest and most crowded yachting centre in this part of the world. Even in the days when *Grayling* sailed the Blackwater there were hundreds of yacht moorings here competing for space in the creeks with the traditional oyster beds, but in addition today there are now several marinas.

Mersea Island was well known to the Romans, who introduced oysters to the area, and of course 'Colchester Natives' have long been famous. But Mersea Island's history goes back much further than the Romans, for the ancient British people had a settlement here, and have left their tumuli behind to prove it. In comparatively modern times King Canute won a great victory nearby over Ethelred's son Edmund Ironsides, and Mersea was also used by the Danes as a retreat and stronghold.

Other battles were fought later in these creeks and inlets between customs officers and smugglers, for smuggling came as second nature to the fishermen of Mersea Island. Smuggling was not always the romantic occupation it is sometimes made out to be, and violence often flared. A particularly gruesome tale is told of one dreadful clash which resulted in a whole boat load of excise officers being found next morning in one of the creeks, each one with his throat cut.

A glance at the chart will reveal some fascinating and intriguing names in and around Mersea Island. The entrance channel from the Blackwater is known as Mersea Quarters, on the starboard hand of which is Cobmarsh Island and the Besom Fleet leading to a landing place at King's Hard. The village here is West Mersea, the northern part of which was — and may still be — known as Mersea City. On the mainland side are some strange names simply asking for an explanation — Old Hall Marsh, Pennyhole Fleet, Quince's Corner (shades of a *Midsummer Night's Dream*!), Joyce's Head, Abbey Hall Marsh, Copthall Saltings, and many others, enough to keep those with an antiquarian turn of mind interested for long enough.

On the south bank of the river below Lawling Creek the terrain is quite different from the north bank, and there is only one creek, at Bradwell. Here there are more yacht moorings and now a marina and today dominating the whole countryside for miles round is the Bradwell Nuclear Power Station. Not everyone agrees that this enhances the natural beauty of the Blackwater River, but as a society we have only ourselves to blame for having created such an insatiable demand for electricity.

But below Bradwell — or Bradwell-juxta-Mare as it was once called — near the mouth of the river on Sales Point is a significant piece of English history in the shape of an old Saxon church, St Peter's-on-the-Wall. Christianity was first brought to these Islands by the Romans, but when they left in AD410 it virtually died out until St Augustine arrived in Kent in 597. From then on churches were built, and St Peter's is thought to be a very early foundation, attributable to St Cedd in 643.

The site of the church however is older, and does go back to the time of the Romans, for it is believed to have once been the Roman settlement of Othona. This was one of the Saxon Shore forts, a chain of them having been established in the third century to cope with the increasing number of raids on south-east England from Germany. Not all experts are agreed that this is the site of Othona, some believing it to have been higher up the coast at Walton, but nevertheless the remains of old Roman walls have been found here. If it is true that this was Othona, then another bloody battle was fought on this spot between Saxons and Romans towards the end of the Roman occupation.

The old Saxon church was for many years used as a barn, but it has since been restored and converted back to being a chapel. In spite of its remoteness services are sometimes held here, though for most of the time it stands alone on the marsh, with only the sea birds, the sea and the sky, and of course the huge and sinister mass of the power station for company. It marks the entrance to one of the most interesting stretches of water on the whole of the East Coast. *Grayling* and her crew were very sorry to have left Kentish waters, but the more we found out about the Blackwater, the Colne, the Crouch and the Roach, and, further up the coast, the Stour and Orwell, the luckier we felt we were.

Merlin

Right Merlin, *Essex-built early this century on the lines of an oyster smack, and registered in Maldon. Her deep draught of 5′ 6″ gave her a good bite on the water and inherent stability, and as a first boat she had much to commend her.*

Below Merlin'*s crew. From left to right, Sally, aged 9, Anthony, aged 11, and my wife. Note the large practical cockpit and the neatly coiled sheets. My wife is peeling the spuds.*

Left *The fifth member of the crew, Mac. He loved* Merlin, *and the sea, as much as we did.*

Below *A friendly party. Many of our friends thought we were mad but came with us out of curiosity. Many were subsequently converted.*

Above Merlin *looked like this when I found her, and it was love at first sight. Over the years she taught me a lot.*

Right *My fault, I'm afraid. We tried to leave the Sandwich river before dawn on Saturday, and I missed one of the buoys in the dark.*

Right *The Coal Board let me lay* Merlin *up on this deserted wharf in the winter. There was no one else within miles, and as I scraped and painted, my only companion was the wind, which was bitter.*

Left Merlin*'s foredeck, on which there was plenty of room, and all her equipment was sturdy and seamanlike. The shrouds were made up on dead eyes which I much prefer to bottle screws.*

Below left *Cockpit and main hatch. Jib and staysail sheets were made up on cleats on the cockpit coaming — a very simple system.*

Above right *Anthony and Sally a year or two later on board the Thames Sailing Barge* Magnet *in Rochester.*

Right *S/B* Magnet, *our floating home for several years. Temporarily alongside is the* Beult, *the Medway Conservancy Board's patrol boat — after all, it was their river we were in.*

MAGNET
AVERSHAM

Left *Moving was fun, and* Magnet *was brought alongside the wharf to receive our personal belongings which came by road. We arrived from Sandwich in* Merlin.

Below left Merlin *in her winter berth by the wharf.* Magnet *can be seen in the background.*

Right *This bleak spot is where we had kept* Merlin *in the Sandwich River Stour, so that our new berth in the Medway represented a considerable change of scene.*

Below Merlin *(the outer boat) in Ramsgate harbour.*

Below right *The crew basking in the sunshine, somewhere off the north Kent coast.*

A gentle sail in the Medway with my mother, aged 88.

Charlie Manley and Anthony (builder and owner) sailing in Mascotte *for the first time.*

Training Ship Arethusa, *which used to be moored at Upnor in the River Medway. She was built in 1911 as the* Peking *for the Chilean nitrate trade.*

Grayling

Built in Brightlingsea in 1900, and originally gaff yawl rigged, Grayling *was changed to sloop later. The difference between* Merlin *and* Grayling *was the difference between a comfortable middle-aged old lady and a high-stepping aristocratic adventuress!* (F.J. Armes)

Above Grayling*'s foredeck, complete with capstan. Originally she had a bowsprit, but this went when her rig was cut down to sloop, which was a pity.*

Below *Broad uncluttered decks, excellent for lounging about, but affording no protection whatsoever from the weather. There was a small, shallow, self-draining cockpit.*

Above *Mast and spider band. From deck to truck her mast measured 56′ 4½″. There was a good view from the top.*

Below Grayling*'s beautiful saloon. Forward, through the door, lay the galley, the loo, and a commodious forecastle.*

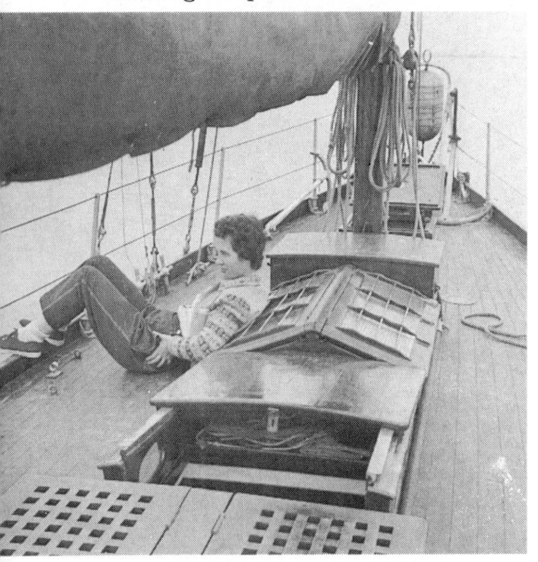

Right *The annual chore, which we all enjoyed. Her hull was a lovely shape, and she made little fuss through the water.*

Below *The long counter was* Grayling*'s weakest point, and the rudder trunking persistently leaked. I was advised to cut the counter off, but this would have ruined her lines.*

Below right *Greasing the track. A head for heights was necessary.*

Left *Ramsgate outer harbour, and time for a scrub.* Grayling *was well named, for she slid through the water like a fish.*

Below *A happy crew in Ramsgate on our way to Ostend. From left to right — Pat, Monk, Sally, Geoff, Jackie and Brian.*

Right *I shall never forget the peace of this summer morning in Brightlingsea. There was no wind and the sun was hot as Monk and I waited for the dew to dry before removing the sail cover.*

Below Grayling *under sail in the Medway. Sally and Pat landed on a huge Admiralty mooring buoy to take this picture.*

Above far left *Taking on bonded stores in Calais, the presence of a gendarme being a legal necessity.*

Above left *Leaving Calais. The entrance can be seen behind us, and the conspicuous lighthouse.*

Left *Skipper and Son.*

Above *Geoff at the helm. The glimpse of the dinghy behind him shows we were travelling at some speed.*

Right *Bird's eye view.*

Calm . . .

. . . Force 3 . . .

. . . Force 5 . . .

. . . Force 8.

Peradventure

Right Peradventure, *a classic 7-ton hull shape by Dr T. Harrison Butler.*

Below *A neat transom and wish-bone bumpkin that followed the line of her sheer.*

7
6
5
4
3
2
1

Left *Sheer magic. A very sturdy but satisfying hull shape that generated tremendous confidence.*

Below left *View showing her cut-away bow and the Wykeham-Martin jib furling gear. Her draught is clearly 4'6".*

Right *Anthony, now a young man, aboard* South Star, *Captain O.M. Watts' MFV in the Beaulieu River.*

Below *Aboard the second Thames Sailing Barge we owned, the* Lord Roberts. *With Anthony is Jim Didhams, an old sailing barge skipper who knew the Thames and Medway inside out, and who skippered the* Lord Roberts *when we raced her.*

Above *The* Lord Roberts *which we bought as a motor barge in trade. Anthony converted her back to sail.*

Left *On the piles at Bucklers Hard. The picture shows the anchor windlass, samson post, bowsprit, and methods of setting jib and staysail.*

Right Peradventure *after the re-fit at the Yard of Messrs Marine Services, Bucklers Hard.*

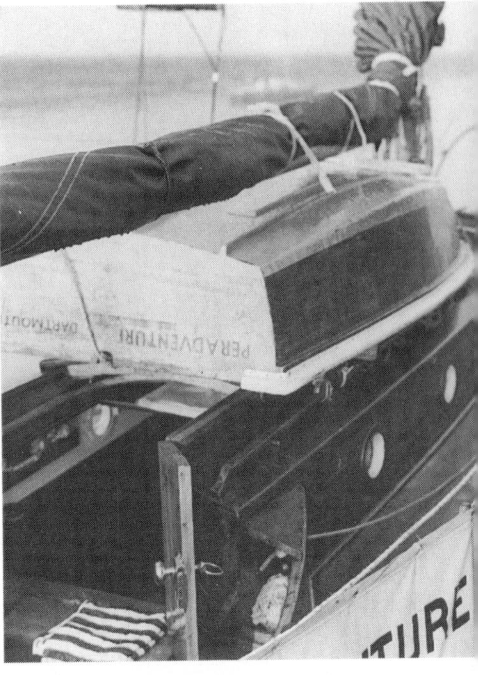

Above left Peradventure*'s foredeck, showing the coach roof brought forward of the mast to give standing headroom in the forecastle.*

Above *We could just get the dinghy aboard, but it was a tight squeeze.*

Left Peradventure*'s saloon was small, but very, very comfortable. We installed a 'Dumpy' coal burning stove and in the winter were very snug.*

Right *The late Captain O.M. Watts, the country's leading Yacht Chandler and Agent. 'Ossie' Watts knew everybody in the yachting world, both here at home and overseas, and everybody loved and respected him.* (Thomson Newspapers)

Right *Entrance to Yarmouth harbour, one of the most attractive small harbours in the country.*

Right *As you come in you see the George Hotel and Yarmouth Castle. When we sailed into Yarmouth our invariable object was dinner at the George.*

Left *Entrance to the Beaulieu River and our mooring a few miles upstream.*

Below *Landing pontoon near our mooring above Bucklers Hard, and typical of the excellent facilities available for yachtsmen in the Beaulieu River.*

Right Peradventure*'s Beaulieu River mooring.*

Below right *Approaching the Marina at Bucklers Hard.*

Above *Skipper.*

Left *Mate.*

Above right *Newtown Creek, the peace of the saltings.*

Right *Clamerkin Lake, Newtown. The other side of the stakes is a marsh, inundated at springs.*

Narija

Left Narija *at sea. There were many happy days of cruising when sea and sky were blue and the sea was calm. It was then that we appreciated the difference between a sailing boat and a motor yacht.*

Below left *Pat at the wheel, revelling in the comfort of the wheelhouse, and enjoying the sense of power that two large diesels gave.*

Above right Narija *on her River Yar mooring, a mile above the town of Yarmouth. A blissful spot.*

Right *In St Katherine's Yachthaven near Tower Bridge, where we spent nearly a year.*

Above *St Katherine's, in the heart of London's East End. Yachts of all shapes and sizes.*

Below *Another part of St Katherine's showing the World Trade Centre on the right which caters for international conferences. The Port of London Authority building can be seen in the background, centre.*

Above Narija *in St Katherine's, Pat's father just stepping aboard. The gentleman in the check shirt standing aft and looking quizzical is our bank manager.*

Below *The old ivory warehouse at St Katherine's has been converted into luxury apartments and we rented one for a time. The views from the windows were not bad.*

Above *The Ivory House as seen from* Narija's *mooring. A Thames Sailing Barge on the left.*

Below *Yarmouth, Isle of Wight, our ultimate home. A picture of the busy harbour.*

13

A modest exploration

THE little village of Latchingdon near Maylandsea had one big advantage for us — it had a pub, called 'The Lion', and this became the rendezvous for *Grayling*'s crew. It was the nearest pub to our mooring and was therefore a convenient meeting place, for we were all arriving by car and from different directions. And so it turned out that on the evening of Friday 7 June 1957 four of us foregathered in the saloon bar at 'The Lion' in preparation for a few days afloat. Brian and Anthony who were both working, Brian in London and Anthony in Rochester, had only the weekend and had to be back not later than Monday, but Geoff and I had a week to look forward to, and meant to enjoy it to the full.

There is always a pleasant sense of anticipation in the air at the beginning of a cruise, particularly when four good friends meet for their first sail of the season together, and though Anthony and I had brought *Grayling* round to Maylandsea a few weeks previously, this was the first time Geoff and Brian had visited her on her new mooring, and I was naturally anxious that they should enjoy themselves. I need not have worried. We had sailed so often together, and the relationship between us was so relaxed and friendly, that whatever the weather and wherever we went, we knew it would be enjoyable.

What with the four of us, our luggage, and a carton of stores, the dinghy had to make two trips down the creek to *Grayling*, but it was a lovely evening, flat calm, with a glow in the sky that presaged a fine day tomorrow, and the tide was full. By 22.00 hours we were all safely aboard and settled in, and had agreed that on the morrow we would make for Brightlingsea, and thence to Pin Mill on the Orwell. Anthony and Brian were happy to leave to chance the problem of how they were to get back to London on Monday.

On Saturday morning the tide went at 09.45 and we planned to carry the ebb all the way down to the Bench Head buoy which marked the confluence of the Blackwater with the river Colne and would keep us in deep water all the way. We were ready by tide time, apart from preparing

the mainsail, so we set the jib, started the engine, and dropped the mooring at 10.00. Within twenty minutes we were in the main river, the mainsail had been hoisted, the engine was shut down, and we were away.

The breeze was not very strong — force 2 from the south-south-east — but it seemed to be freshening, and *Grayling* obviously liked the conditions for she covered the first three miles downstream at a speed of six knots. There were one or two yachts proceeding in the same direction, and our log has a rather smug entry —

Breeze now force 3. Passing everything in sight.

One of the delights in sailing in this particular little ship was that in anything from force 3 upwards she was very fast, and when in addition the water was calm she slid through it like a fish. Only when it was rough did you get soaked on deck.

By 11.30 we were doing so well, with the Bench Head well in sight, that I decided to cut the corner and make for the Inner Bench Head buoy which is off Colne Point. This involved crossing over a long narrow sandbank, but at this state of the tide there was plenty of water. We were now able to free our sheets for the run up the Colne, as our course had changed from south-east to north-east, but speed over the ground dropped dramatically for instead of having the ebb under us we were now punching it. From the Inner Bench Head to the buoy marking the entrance to Brightlingsea Creek is only about two miles, but it took us three-quarters of an hour.

Brightlingsea entrance is shallow and tricky, there being only about 4 ft of water on the bar at low water springs, but there was still about four hours of ebb left, so there were no problems and we sailed in in great style. There were no passengers in this crew and by the time we reached the moorings off the town hard sails were down and furled, mooring warps were in position, and we moored up alongside a large motor cruiser called *Annanetta* in an atmosphere of professional calm, which did the Skipper's heart good.

Brightlingsea, or Bricklesea as it was once called, is an ancient port, its record going back at least to the 14th century. In 1442 it became a 'limb' of the Cinque Port of Sandwich, of all places, and in 1589 there is a record of fourteen Brightlingsea men having served with Sir Francis Drake. All through the centuries the town has had a reputation for producing brave and fearless sailors, whether local fishermen or deep sea, and in his book *Last Stronghold of Sail* Harvey Benham tells some blood-curdling stories of their toughness and bravery in appalling weather conditions.

The Brightlingsea fishing fleet reached its peak in the 19th century when there were over 200 smacks in the town, many of them being cutters built by the local firm of Aldous. All Aldous-built smacks were supplied complete with a Bible and a box in the cabin in which to keep it, and though not all sailors conform to the conventional image of a God-fearing man, there are few who have not been impressed by the awe-inspiring fury and power of the sea.

Our short stay in Brightlingsea passed all too quickly, we went ashore to stretch our legs, and entertained Harold Day, the Harbour Master, aboard. On the top of the tide, in bright moonlight, we left the town for Pyefleet Creek on the other side of the river, so that in the morning we could get away whenever we pleased. The entrance to Pyefleet is a sheltered and quiet anchorage, and was one of our favourites. The log entry says:

22.45 Dropped hook in Pyefleet. Peace.

When we got up in the morning the peace of Pyefleet that we had felt the night before was still there. It was a typical Sunday morning, bright and clear — perhaps a little too bright to be settled — and there was a quietness in the air that one does not get on a working day. After breakfast Anthony and I went on deck waiting for the other two to join us. We both felt the urge to be on our way, so we quietly pulled up the anchor, started the engine and motored out of the creek. Once in the river we got sail on her and shut down the motor, and for three-quarters of an hour had a blissful and silent sail, the wind being southerly, force 3. Unfortunately we then had to resort to the engine again as the wind gradually headed us, and against the flood tide we could make no progress.

After plugging doggedly into the wind and tide for another hour we reached the Colne Bar buoy, where at last we were able to alter course to port and steer for the North Eagle buoy and then Priory Spit. Here we really felt we were getting somewhere for we could now quite clearly see Clacton Pier which was only a couple of miles further on.

The first four miles from Pyefleet to Colne Bar had taken an hour and fifty minutes, which means that our speed over the ground was a miserable 2.2 knots. From this point on *Grayling*'s log records some figures of the times taken for the rest of the journey, and I reproduce these with some diffidence since they show that my estimates were not very accurate:

	ETA	*Actual*	*Miles*	*Approx Speed*
Colne Bar	10.00	10.20		
Priory Spit	10.45	10.50	2½	5 knots
Clacton Pier	11.20	11.18	2½	5 knots
Walton Pier	13.00	12.15	6½	6 knots
Medusa Buoy	13.20	12.30	1½	6 knots
Stone Banks Buoy	13.45	12.50	2	6 knots
Landguard Point	14.30	13.20	3	6 knots
Pin Mill	16.00	14.30	6	5 knots

In mitigation perhaps it may be said that I had anticipated much less wind than we found, and in the event our average speed was fairly respectable. We had a few drops of rain as we passed Clacton about a mile and a half off the land and a thunderstorm was travelling north over the town, parallel to our course. There seemed to be several other thunderstorms about, and the wind was a little fluky, but about force 4-5 with occasional lulls. From the Medusa buoy onwards we were on a dead run, and now and again gybed.

12.50 Stone Banks abeam after two gybes. Going like a train.
13.20 Entered Harwich Harbour, the last few miles being most exhilarating. A dead run with the jib goose-winged. Wind force 4 gusting to 5. Quarter wave up to the gunwale, and a noise like Niagara. Dinghy planing.

This last experience was quite extraordinary, and had I not known *Grayling*'s underwater shape I should have thought she was planing. As it was she 'squatted' on to her counter, her bow went up in the air, and she surged along as though she was surf riding.

I was reminded of this incident the next time I came into Harwich in *Grayling*, for in exactly the same spot where she had started to surf we were hit by a sudden vicious black squall which blotted out the land and everything else around us. After hurriedly reefing, and in torrential rain which reduced visibility to almost nil, we turned to the east and ran before it until it was over.

But on the present occasion we proceeded swiftly on our way and dropped anchor off Pin Mill at 14.30. We had passed two boats further back, *Maid of Corris* and *Yara*, and when they came in they anchored quite close to us. Actually we had passed *Maid of Corris* off Clacton where she had been inshore of us, and at first looking at her through the binoculars I had only been able to make out the words '*Maid of C . . .*' which was immediately interpreted as 'Made of Cardboard' — and this naturally became her nickname.

The afternoon was passed in a round of social engagements and the crews of both the boats near us were invited aboard, followed by us being invited aboard them. Ultimately, having made a number of new friends we all went ashore for a drink at the 'Butt and Oyster'.

We found the 'Butt and Oyster' rather disappointing. Its fame had led us to expect something special, but it seemed to us to be rather lacking in character. It was busy at the time but the staff did not seem terribly interested in their customers. So we walked half a mile up the road in the rain to the other pub in Chelmondiston (or Chempston, we were told). This pub, the 'Riga' was of a very different type, smaller, less pretentious, with the walls of the bar covered with old photographs of 'J' Class yachts, and it was obviously the favourite haunt of elderly locals. We talked to one old man who claimed to have sailed in the 'J' Class, each of which had a crew of 25. The 'Riga' seemed somehow to be more genuine than the 'Butt and Oyster'.

The following morning, after a night of continuous rain, we got our anchor and proceeded upstream to Ipswich in order to put Anthony and Brian on to a train. They were both reluctant to go, but duty called, Anthony having to go to Rochester via London, and Brian to Maylandsea via Chelmsford to pick up his car. Geoff and I were left to spend a few more days in *Grayling*, and to get her back to her mooring in Maylandsea by the end of the week.

★ ★ ★

Ipswich Docks on a wet Monday morning are not among the most romantic spots on earth, and the place where we were temporarily moored while Geoff put Anthony and Brian ashore in the dinghy was filthy and smelled rather badly. So we were glad to get away and sail back down the lovely Orwell River. Many people have compared the Orwell to the Beaulieu River and there are many similarities, both rivers being surrounded by most attractive countryside, with woods coming down to the waters edge, and each having a charming village to visit — Bucklers Hard in the Beaulieu River, and Pin Mill in the Orwell. The principal difference is that the Orwell has more mud, and though the channel is dredged and buoyed you have to watch your step.

It was a gentle sail down as far as Pin Mill with a rather fitful breeze, and as the channel was narrow we used the engine. The weather looked far from promising, clouds being low and grey, and it seemed inevitable that there was more rain to come. We talked about where we should go and as Geoff expressed a wish to visit Wrabness on the Stour, where he had friends, we decided not to stop at Pin Mill but to press on.

We now had another six miles to go downstream before reaching Harwich harbour, and Geoff went down below, leaving me alone to sail *Grayling*. He said afterwards that he did this deliberately, as he felt it would do me good to be on my own for a bit, and I regarded this as a very kind thought — although I suppose it could have meant that I had been getting on his nerves! But I must say it was a thoroughly enjoyable and restful hour as *Grayling* glided quietly down the river.

Off Shotley Point a lightship was moored and it was necessary to gybe as we rounded it, and this brought Geoff up from below as we went tearing up the Stour past Parkeston Quay in a temporary puff. Then the breeze died away completely and it started to rain heavily, so we had to put on our oillies, start the engine, and hand the sails.

The Stour, which is the county boundary between Essex and Suffolk, is nothing like as attractive as the Orwell as a sailing river, and it has even more mud. It is surrounded by beautiful countryside, much of which was the inspiration of both Gainsborough and Constable, but with a deep-keeled boat one has to be very careful indeed. At high water the river appears to be over a mile wide all the way from Harwich to Wrabness, a distance of about five miles, but the navigable channel at low water narrows from about half a mile off Shotley to only one cable at Wrabness.

We dropped anchor at Wrabness at 16.15 in 2½ fathoms, the last half mile or so being a struggle against a very strong ebb. The tide was sluicing out through the narrows and we had a very hard row to get ashore, and we paused on the beach to watch a woman in a dinghy who was having the greatest difficulty in making it back to her boat. For a time we thought we might have to go and rescue her, but she made it in the end.

Our destination was the village pub where Geoff knew the landlord's daughter and her husband. Here we had a pleasant yarn with them and watched some of the locals nonchalently playing incredibly skilful darts. On the way back to the boat we wandered up the sandy beach to the local chalet and caravan park — not a particularly pretty sight. In fact, drab Wrabness!

The following day showed a complete change in the weather — for the better — and we had a glorious day's sailing on our way back to Brightlingsea. The ship's log actually says it all:

> A bright windy day, visibility excellent in complete contrast to yesterday. Wind force 5-6 and a fair wind for the Colne. Spent a lazy morning pottering about. Met a butcher on the beach and bought some bangers.
>
> 14.20 Got the anchor and went roaring downstream on jib and engine. Wind NW force 5. HW 12.05. Hoisted mainsail with difficulty and shut down engine. Wind tending to slacken, but several squalls.
>
> 15.00 Exactly 3 o'clock as we passed a clock tower on the way out of Harwich harbour.
>
> 15.20 Cliff End buoy. Wind not more than force 3 at most. A dead run to Stone Banks buoy. Hot sunshine, calm sea. Jib goosewinged, and a trade-winds roll!
>
> 15.50 Stone Banks abeam. Gybed just before reaching it.
>
> 16.10 Gybed round to south-west.
>
> 16.25 Crossed line of Naze Tower and Medusa buoy. Latter about 1 mile distant.
>
> 16.50 Walton Pier abeam.
>
> 17.05 Wind freshening and a thunderstorm gathering over the land. Tucked in a reef.
>
> 17.30 A fearsome sky has built up and over the land it is very dark with the rain falling like a curtain. Tucked down some more sail.
>
> 17.45 Handed the jib as it was not doing any good. We may be lucky and miss the centre of the storm as it appears to be travelling faster than us and passing round ahead of us.

18.10 Clacton Pier abeam. A few drops of rain only, and main storm is now on our port hand out at sea. Vivid forked lightning. Saw what could only have been a waterspout about 2 miles away.

18.30 The wind suddenly fell right away and left us wallowing in a slightly lumpy sea. Started the engine but only had to use it for 5 minutes when a smart little breeze came away from the north.

18.45 Priory Spit buoy abeam. Sailing well again.

19.10 Colne Bar buoy. Stood on for half a mile and then started to beat up Colne. Hove-to and got most of reef out. Geoff amazed at the process of heaving-to! This turned out to be a very enjoyable sail in the evening sunshine with the wind gradually dropping. A Colchester smack passed us, and also *Nellie*, one of Tony Lapthorn's barges. Practised going about smartly.

20.30 Entered Brightlingsea Creek on engine — wondering whether there was enough water to get in.

20.32 No! Kedged her off.

21.15 Moored up on the trot opposite the Hard. A perfect summer evening at last.

	ETA	*Actual*
Walton Pier	17.00	16.50
Clacton Pier	18.20	18.10
Priory Spit	19.00	18.45
Colne Bar	19.35	19.10
Brightlingsea	20.30	20.30

Actually the sail up the river from the Colne Bar to Brightlingsea was little short of magical. The water was flat calm, there was very little wind, and there was such a stillness and feeling of peace in the air that we found ourselves talking in whispers. We not only practiced going about smartly but also silently, so as not to disturb the peace of the evening. For me this was what sailing was all about, and I am grateful for the fact that a vivid memory of the experience has stayed with me over the years.

After this I quite expected the rest to be an anti-climax, but funnily enough on the following morning the magic was still there. We were off at 05.00 to catch the last of the ebb out of Brightlingsea and just managed to get out with literally a few inches of water under our keel. By 06.00 we were abeam of the Bench Head buoy and passed two Colchester smacks trawling. The two fishermen were having a conversation, and though they were at least a quarter of a mile away from us, in the still clear air we could hear every word. Half an hour later the log says:

> 06.35 Geoff produced a steaming hot mug of tea, very acceptable, as although the sun was warm the breeze was chilly. Not a cloud in the sky and high overhead it was dark blue against the red and white of the sails. Sea like a millpond and visibility excellent — why don't we always get up at 4.45 am?

At 07.55 we anchored off Stone St Lawrence and had breakfast in the hot sunshine and perfect peace, after which we lazed our way back to Maylandsea and our home mooring, thoroughly contented.

14

Youth at the helm

WHEN you are addicted to sailing, and own your own boat, there is a regrettable tendency to be selfish and only reluctantly let someone else have the helm. With me this started the first day I was introduced to sailing when I was invited to helm a friend's boat on the Norfolk Broads, and I have suffered from the disease ever since. Fortunately there are photographs available showing members of my family and also various friends at the tiller of the boats I have owned, and these help a little to assuage my guilty conscience, but it was always a bit of a battle to give up the helm to someone else.

Except to the children. It was obvious that if only for safety reasons they should become proficient at handling the boat, and consequently they learned the rudiments at an early age. By the time they were in their teens they could hold their own with anyone, not only in steering, but in handling the sails, in anchoring, and in picking up a mooring. The log records a typical incident at a time when Sally was fifteen. We had been sailing for the weekend — Sally, Pat, Geoff, Monk, and I — and had picked up a mooring close to the T.S. *Arethusa* at Upnor while we had tea. When it was time for us to go back to our own mooring in Gillingham the girls decided that they wanted to handle the boat.

17.45 Dropped moorings and down stream to Gillingham. Sally and Pat on deck, Geoff, Monk, and I confined down below!
18.10 Sal and Pat pick up the buoy by themselves first time! No comment!

Later, Sally's schoolfriend Jackie sailed with us on several occasions, and she too became proficient and a useful member of the crew. And of course Anthony's two-year stint as the mate of a Thames sailing barge qualified him as a professional, for there had been occasions when he had sailed his barge single-handed, and hence handling a boat the size of *Grayling* presented no problems at all. So that when the opportunity

arose for a cruising holiday on which I could not be present all the time I had no qualms in letting Anthony take charge. I knew he could handle the boat, I just wondered if he could also handle his younger sister and her friend.

Sally and Jackie came over to Essex from Kent and stayed the night at my flat in Harlow New Town, and the following morning we picked up Anthony and Brian at Chelmsford station on the way down to Maylandsea. It was blowing hard and the creek was choppy so we accepted gratefully a tow down to *Grayling*'s mooring, but even so we were pretty wet by the time we got aboard.

The tide went at 12.15 and the creek then became calmer, but the wind was a good force 6 from slightly south of west and we made a very fast passage to Brightlingsea. It was a wet sail as the sea was rough, and some yachtsman must have been in trouble somewhere for off the mouth of the Colne we met the Clacton lifeboat returning home. As we went into Brightlingsea we passed the sailing barge *Leonard Piper*, and the mate shouted to us that we should go aground on the course we were on, which was kind of him, though in fact he was wrong.

Perhaps he was clairvoyant though, for when we got to the town we found the wind had blown the moorings hard to one side, and we did in fact go aground. The tide was falling and we hurriedly put our patent drill into operation, and with anchors attached to the halyards on each side —

and occasionally hoisting the jib — we managed to keep *Grayling* upright. We were almost the only boat to be in this happy position for the moorings had been blown over so far to the north that there was practically no water at all at low tide.

We gave the bottom a good scrub, and on the next high water moved to a deeper mooring so that we were able to stay afloat. It was a very good thing we did move, for the weather worsened and we had almost 48 hours of strong gales. At one point it was so rough that we could not get ashore, and saw several dinghies capsize. But we were very snug and comfortable. When the weather moderated we had a visit from our old friend Harold Day, the Queen's Harbour Master, and also from Peter Hills, a Trinity House pilot, so were not lacking in social engagements and interesting conversation.

We had a small library of sailing books aboard *Grayling*, including the first volume of Frank Cowper's *Sailing Tours*, published in 1892. In this book he describes how he set out from London and sailed along the Essex and Suffolk coasts entering every inlet, river and creek that would take a boat with a draught of 6 ft. In the preface he states that if the book proved successful he would go on and circumnavigate Great Britain with the same methodical intention. The book is most interesting as a picture of what yachting was like 100 years ago when there were very few yachts about, and it must have been successful for he went on and completed the job, the last of several volumes being dated 1896.

As soon as the gales abated we left Brightlingsea and set off for the Orwell and Pin Mill, and for three days had some delightful sailing in very changeable but typical English summer weather. After Pin Mill we visited Wrabness and the log records that while at anchor there we had a celebration dinner, it being three years to the day since we had our first sail in *Grayling*.

On the morrow we returned to the Colne as the time was approaching when Brian and I had to leave and return to London, so we let the children take over, starting with getting the anchor up. With Anthony on the tiller and engine controls the two girls tackled the anchor, which they found unexpectedly difficult. I was aft with Anthony and Brian was up forward watching the girls' efforts, when suddenly the anchor broke out and Sally and Jackie collapsed in a giggling heap on the deck.

'Come on!' I said, rather sharply, 'Tell us when the anchor is clear.'

Brian very calmly turned to me and said:

'Confucious say that when anchor crew flat on back with anchor chain in hand, anchor is clear!'

After that they had no trouble, sailed her into Brightlingsea immaculately, and moored up alongside another yacht 'without breaking an egg'.

At 06.10 the following morning Anthony put Brian and I ashore to catch the 6.38 train to town, and within twenty minutes of landing us on the hard he, and perhaps a rather sleepy crew, had *Grayling* sailing out of Brightlingsea Creek. When I joined the ship again a few days later it was to find her in immaculate condition, cleaner than I had seen her for a long time, and with ropes coiled down in true naval fashion. I might have known that as I stepped aboard the blue ensign would be hoisted.

Somehow this seemed to signal the end of an era — and the beginning of a new one.

PART 3

PERADVENTURE

I know not why I yearn for you again,
To sail once more upon thy fickle flood;
I'll hear thy waves wash under my death-bed,
Thy salt is lodged forever in my blood.

WILLIAM HENRY DAVIES

15

The Harrison-Butler 7-tonners

OUR last cross-Channel trip in *Grayling* is memorable to me — for two reasons. I had already decided to sell her, for what later seemed to be totally inadequate reasons, and we all knew that this was probably the last time we should all be sailing together. There was a sort of feeling of reckless despair in the air, a feeling I hope never to experience again, and I pushed *Grayling* to her limit.

It was blowing very hard — force 6 to 7 — the sky was deep blue, and the sea had that wonderful almost black look, with whiter than white breaking crests to the waves, the whole surface of the sea being streaked with white. It had been rough for some days and we passed several large patches of seaweed that had been torn off some beach or other by the pounding of the waves.

But what made the crossing memorable was, firstly, that our time from Dover pierheads to Calais pierheads was exactly three hours, or an average of just over 7 knots, and when *Grayling* was travelling at this sort of speed in a rough sea she scooped up lots of water, and so we all got very wet. It was wild, it was exciting, it was magnificent. On the weather side of the ship the rigging was bar taut, thrumming in the wind like the strings of a musical instrument, and the whole ship was vibrating with life and energy.

The other thing I remember, and shall never forget, was that when we sailed up Calais harbour in the suddenly quietened water Brian came up to me as I stood on the foredeck. His oillies were dripping with water, his face was glistening, and his eyebrows were caked with salt which gave him an unwontedly fierce expression.

'You are a bloody fool' he said, 'to sell this boat'.

I don't think I ever heard Brian swear either before or since but on this occasion he was blazing. Unhappily I knew that he was right, though it did not stop me going ahead with my plans, and it was nearly ten years before I owned another small sailing boat.

Not that I was completely out of touch with the water during that period, for Anthony and I went into partnership and bought a Thames spritsail barge, the *Lord Roberts*, with the object of doing some charter work. When we bought her she was trading as a motor barge, having had all her sailing gear stripped out of her, and Anthony set about converting her back to sail. In this partnership he was very much the senior since he understood and loved sailing barges, but I was able to help with the paperwork and also with the conversion of her hold into sleeping accommodation, though I am no carpenter. When some years later we sold her it was with my share that I was able to think about buying another boat, this time in partnership with Pat Withams who had crewed so many times in *Grayling*.

By this time I through my friendship with Captain O.M. Watts of Albemarle Street (for whom Pat was working) had met Pat Russell, owner of a small boatyard in Hythe on Southampton Water. Pat Russell also had another small yacht yard in the Beaulieu River at Buckler's Hard, and was the owner of *Ardglass*, a Harrison-Butler 7-tonner.

Fifty years ago the name of Harrison-Butler was well known in yachting circles in this country, and was synonymous with all that was best in yacht design. Working in the days before fibreglass had been developed for small boat construction he was a craftsman in wood. He was also a perfectionist and all the hulls he designed were sturdy, and had a great beauty of line. When something *looks* right, then very often it *is* right, and there is no doubt that all his designs had the thoroughbred look.

His particular interest was in balance and ease of handling, and he strove to correct the prevailing characteristic of many yachts of carrying heavy weather helm. In this he was conspicuously successful. Most of his designs were of small boats, his most popular size being around 7 tons Thames Measurement. It is a feature of all his designs that they will sail to windward under all plain sail without attention to the tiller, and there are not many modern GRP yachts that can claim this.

Ardglass was one of his earliest 7-tonners, built in 1929 by Anderson, Rigden and Perkins of Whitstable, with a waterline length of 22.5 ft and LOA 25.5 ft, a beam of 8.5 ft and a draft of 4 ft 6 in. Basically we were looking for a small auxiliary cruising yacht, preferably with character and some degree of comfort, and suitable for modest coastwise and cross-Channel cruises. Though she was not on the market *Ardglass* obviously fulfilled this specification and her type interested us. When Pat Russell kindly suggested we should take her away for a week we jumped at the offer.

We picked her up from his yard in Hythe, where she had been fitting out, and at the end of the week delivered her to her mooring in the

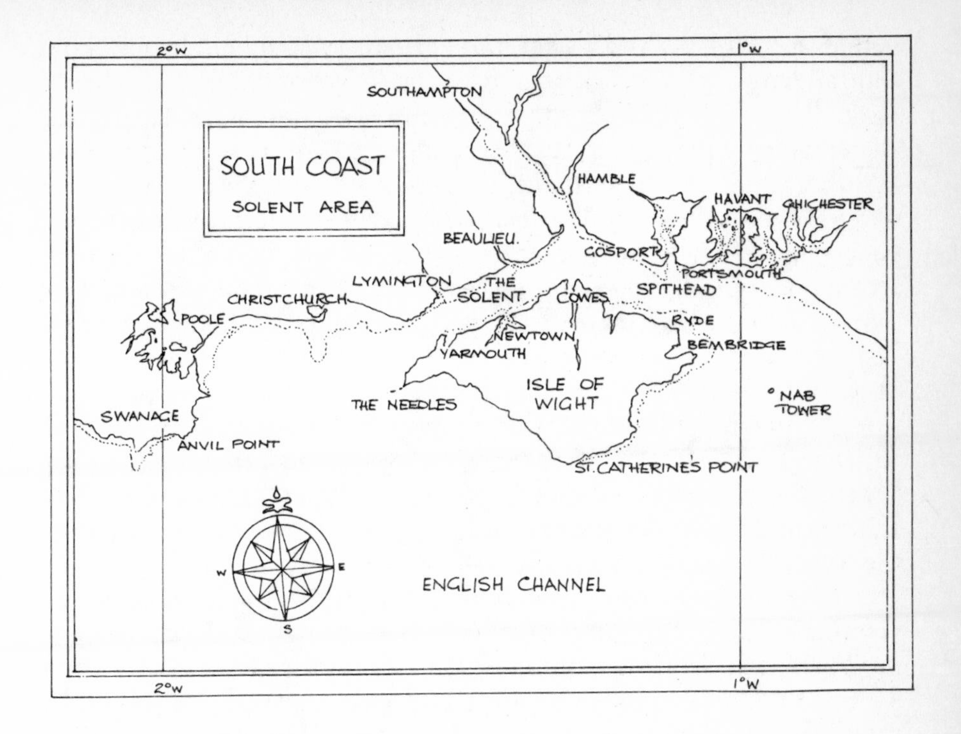

Beaulieu River above Buckler's Hard. This was our first experience of a Harrison-Butler boat, and from the start we were delighted. We were not expecting a high performance, but *Ardglass* was easy to sail. Her gear was not too heavy to handle, and her balance was good. Even in a blow she carried very little weather helm, and we spent three or four days blissfully cruising in and out of the Solent, fetching up each night in the peace and quiet of Newtown.

On arrival back in the Beaulieu River we were already ardent Harrison-Butler fans, and had decided — perhaps somewhat presumptuously — that we were going to own a 7-tonner, come what may. Pat Russell was sympathetic about our aims, which he thoroughly endorsed, but declined to part with *Ardglass*, so we had to look elsewhere.

Our search for another 7-tonner was systematic and reasonably thorough. From the current Lloyds Register we listed all the Harrison-Butler 7-tonners there were, a total of nineteen in all, and then began to put them in order of preference. Some were more difficult of access than others, for example one was in Toronto, one was in Sark, and several were in Ireland. But many of them were local, and very quickly we came down to a short list of eight, our plan then being to tackle all the owners in order,

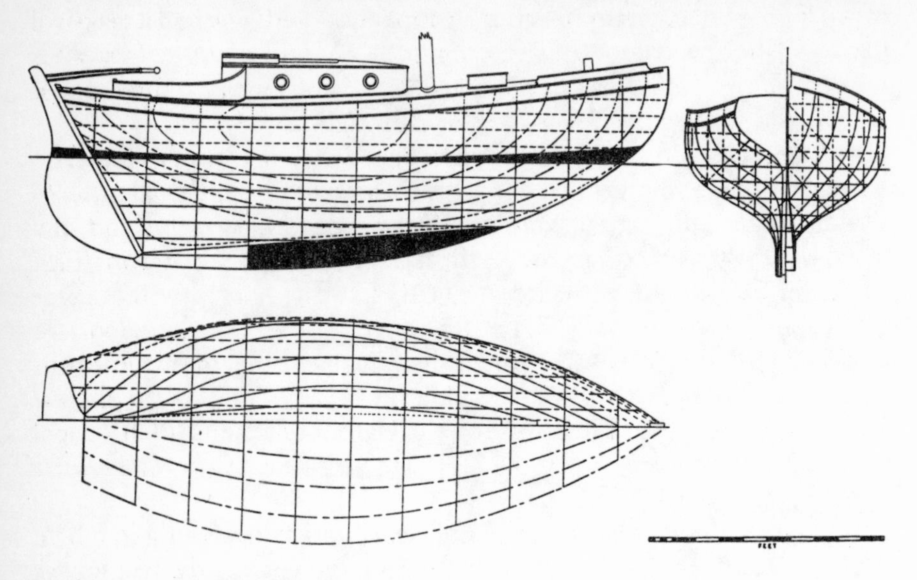

Peradventure *was built to these lines.*

with a view to a sale. From the start we were confident that one of them would agree.

At the head of our list was *Peradventure*, a boat of considerable character, and with vital statistics very similar to *Ardglass*. Her waterline length was the same but she had slightly longer overhangs, and her depth was rather less. In spite of this latter dimension she had somewhat more headroom than *Ardglass* and was generally a little more lush down below.

She was designed in 1936 on the lines of the famous *Englyn* and built for a very tall man, Ewan Montague, who was Recorder for Middlesex, and who achieved additional fame during the war as the author of a plan to deceive the Germans about our invasion intentions, a plan ultimately made into a film under the name of *The Man Who Never Was*.

We contacted the owner of *Peradventure* who lived near Lymington, and who surprised and delighted us by at least agreeing to discuss the possibility of a sale. Negotiations took a little while, and by the time the sale was agreed the sailing season had passed and *Peradventure* was laid up ashore at Webster's Yard in Lymington. One cold and draughty day that winter Anthony and I carried out a survey on her hull, and could find very little wrong. It was forthwith confirmed with the owner that we would buy her, and in due course, though not until the following September, she became ours.

Peradventure had also been built by Anderson, Rigden and Perkins of pitch pine on oak frames, and was copper fastened. She had a teak-laid deck and her coachroof and exterior trim were all of teak. Her sheer rejoiced the eye, and her bowsprit carried the line along, so that both at anchor and underway she looked the thoroughbred she was.

Down below her cabin trim was in oak, which made for a very warm and comfortable saloon. The fo'c'sle was separated from the saloon by a sliding door, on the back of which was fitted a collapsible wash-stand, and in her day this was considered to be the latest thing. The fo'c'sle contained a built-in bunk on the starboard side, with drawers under, as well as a pipe cot to port, and the Baby Blake sea toilet. Just inside the saloon we installed a 'Dumpy' coal stove, and indeed Pat lived aboard for some time on a Beaulieu River mooring just off Marine Services Yard, where she was able to help our friend Billy Grindey, the Harbour Master, with his paper work. Ultimately we moved upstream to a mooring next to *Peradventure*'s more elderly relative *Ardglass*.

This was the beginning of several years' satisfying sailing in a boat which, though small, was extremely comfortable and handy. In a seaway she behaved impeccably, and even when it was rough and she was standing on her ear one never felt the slightest qualm at the possibility of losing control. When the wind failed she had a 9-hp two-cylinder Stuart Turner two-stroke diesel, a somewhat uncommon but highly reliable motor which had the great merit of starting easily and promptly when required. All in all, *Peradventure* was a boat of great character.

Many of the boats built to this design in the 1930s, and now over fifty years old, are still hale and hearty, and continue to give their owners great pleasure. They are a tribute to the skill of their builders and to the designing genius of the late Dr Tom Harrison-Butler. Were he still alive today it is interesting to speculate on the contribution he might have made to GRP design.

★ ★ ★

Peradventure's mooring in the Beaulieu River was little short of idyllic. About a mile above the tiny hamlet of Buckler's Hard, where there was a shop, a garage, a pub, and a little yacht yard, the woods of Keeping Copse come right down to the river's left bank. Here there was a wooden jetty and a landing pontoon which was afloat at all states of the tide, and in the woods at the back a clearing for use as a car park. The river contained a single line of swinging moorings, and I suppose not more than a couple of dozen yachtsmen used this landing stage, so that the place was blissfully quiet.

It was thus possible to bring the car to within a few yards of the landing, and yet it could not be seen or heard from the river, which is an ideal arrangement. From here it was a pleasant half-mile walk across the fields back to Buckler's Hard, or in the other direction about two miles up to Beaulieu itself through delightful woodland.

Beaulieu is well named, and many have claimed that in an area renowned for the quiet beauty of its scenery, this is the prettiest spot of all. It received its name from the monks of Citeaux who founded an abbey here in 1204, following a clash with King John, the story being told that after the King had threatened violence to the monks, he then experienced a very frightening dream in which the monks were scourging him severely, and in order to prevent the dream from coming true he gave them land on which to build an abbey. Not only did he give them the land but he gave them unprecedented rights over it, including ownership of the bed of the river and foreshore, which normally remain the property of the Crown. These rights have descended with the property down to the present owner, Lord Montagu of Beaulieu, and thankfully the land has so far escaped being developed.

With her draft of 4 ft 6 in *Peradvenutre* could, with care, leave her mooring at low water, though of course it was usual to set sail nearer high tide time so as to use the ebb for extra speed in getting down the river. Between the mooring and Buckler's Hard there was a huge S-bend in the river with yacht moorings all the way, and nowadays with a marina on the starboard hand with fuelling berth and modern facilities for lifting out.

Only once did we lay *Peradventure* up ashore. She was lifted out by the very efficient Renner hoist and chocked up, and it was certainly easier to work on her during the winter, but the operation obviously strained her for it took us the whole of the next season to cure various deck and coachroof leaks. After that experience we kept her afloat — in the element for which she had been designed — and thoroughly enjoyed the bad weather which our 'Dumpy' coal stove completely counteracted. There is something peculiarly satisfying about being snug and warm down below when up top the wind is trying to blow the mast out of the boat and the rain is lashing down. As well as our radio we had a tape recorder and a number of classical tapes, from Vivaldi, Bach and Beethoven to Sid Phillips and Dave Brubeck, and we lacked nothing in the way of either spiritual or temporal comfort.

And of course when the fine weather came and the leaves were on the trees what better spot could there be? Indeed there were times, especially if there was no wind, when the temptation to stay put could not be resisted, and sailing had to be postponed in favour of doing some of the many jobs that always need doing on a boat. But when we did leave the mooring we had the fascinating prospect of a six-mile sail down to the mouth of the river, and as this is one of the prettiest rivers in the country this was always interesting.

Buckler's Hard is a strange little place with an interesting history. It was laid out in the early 18th century by the Duke of Montague, the owner of the land, who intended to build a sugar refinery there — he also owned the island of St Lucia in the West Indies — but this project came to naught, and it was not until the wars with Napoleon came along that a use was found for it. During these wars however it became a thriving centre of the ship-building industry and many large warships were built there, including the *Agamemnon, Swiftsure*, and *Euryalus*, all of which fought at Trafalgar. The master builder was one Henry Adams and his house nearby is now an hotel, still called 'The Master Builder's House'.

Below Buckler's Hard the river widens and the moorings thicken for a distance of well over two miles, the river passing a number of large houses, each with its own landing stage. The lower down the river the larger and more opulent are the yachts on the moorings, some being very well known boats indeed. In our day perhaps the most famous was *Gypsy Moth III* belonging to a renowned yachtsman, Sir Francis Chichester. A little lower down still, just below the Royal Southampton Yacht Club's clubhouse and opposite Gin's Farm, was Captain Watts' 54-ft MFV *South Star.*

On the next bend in the river, Needs Oar Point, is a shallow channel to starboard connecting the river with the Solent and usable by shoal draft craft on the tide, and below this is Beaulieu Spit, a large expanse of marsh and sand, awash at high tide, which is a bird sanctuary. At its mouth the Beaulieu River turns sharp to starboard and empties into the Solent, and from here the yachtsman has a wide range of attractive anchorages to visit without ever leaving the shelter of the Isle of Wight.

We had two particular favourites, especially if time was short, for they were both close at hand, namely the Newtown River and Yarmouth. Newtown is unique and is, I believe, the only completely unspoilt and undeveloped harbour on the south coast, much of it being owned by the National Trust and designated a nature reserve. The river entrance is comparatively easy in daylight hours, and once inside there are four arms, rather like the fingers of a hand. Each one is different and has its own character, and though there is not a lot of water it is usually possible to find somewhere to anchor and remain afloat at all states of the tide.

Up one of the arms is a small stone-built quay where it is possible

to leave the dinghy and walk the mile or so into Shalfleet, where there is a pub. Another arm has a rather rickety jetty landing place, and from here there is a short walk to Lower Hamstead Farm where there is a shop selling all necessities. Water is obtainable here too, so that the weekend yachtsman is well catered for, and as a result at holiday weekends Newtown can become very crowded.

But the true beauty of Newtown is in mid-week or out of season when there are few boats about, for then one can appreciate its wildness, its remoteness from civilization, and the dominance of sky and sea and marsh. It was once an important island town and sent two members to Parliament in Westminster, but in 1377 it was visited by the French who destroyed it, and Newtown never recovered from this blow. Today there are a few scattered cottages and an ancient town hall, but the line of some of the old streets can still be seen in the fields.

Yarmouth is even older than Newtown and is entirely different, in an equally fascinating and charming way. Yarmouth was built as a town on the grid system in the 12th century, and for many years was the principal town and port in the island. Built on a peninsula of land it has never been able to grow and sprawl like so many old towns, so that it still preserves its old world charm, in spite of the fact that it is now a busy ferry port connecting with Lymington on the mainland. An indication of its long history, and its one-time importance in the scheme of things, is that it has over the centuries been granted no fewer than seven charters — whereas most towns regard it as a proud achievement if they acquire just one. Yarmouth has had a mayor since 1440.

The harbour is, and always has been, the centre of activity in

Yarmouth. It is small, but accommodates several hundred yachts as well as the busy car ferry service to the mainland. It is delightful in every way. The George Hotel, once the home of the governor of the island, is near the quay, and was a favourite port of call of ours for dinner on a Saturday night. Over the years since our introduction to the Solent area we became so attached to Yarmouth that when I retired we made it our home.

Peradventure was also very much at home in Yarmouth and Newtown, and all the other Solent harbours. She was well-known in these waters, and wherever she went along this stretch of the south coast she was recognized, and people commented on her beautiful lines.

★ ★ ★

The bar in the Royal Lymington Yacht Club is a very comfortable and friendly room, and never was it more so than on the day we took delivery of *Peradventure*. This was a day that both Pat and I had looked forward to impatiently for many months, in fact ever since the previous winter when Anthony and I had surveyed *Peradventure*, and the owner had agreed to a sale. And now it was September, another sailing season had been lost, and she was still not ours.

The sale had not gone through as smoothly as we had hoped, the agreement reached with the owner last February being that he would put her in the water and fit her out, towards the cost of which I would

contribute an extra £100, and we would be able to take her away in April. But alas for the schemes of mice and men. In March the owner rang me, full of apologies, to ask for a little more time. Apparently his son had secured a place in an American University, commencing in September, and was anxious to have one more sailing season in *Peradventure* before he went. Would I mind delaying taking the boat over until August.

Actually I minded very much, but could see his point of view and reluctantly agreed to a postponement, on condition that the sale should be completed and the boat handed over by 31 August. This was agreed, and Pat and I resigned ourselves, not very happily, to yet another summer without a boat.

August came, and August nearly went, without any word from the owner, and ultimately I phoned him to find out the arrangements for handing over. Blandly he informed me that he had put the boat on the market and she was now in the hands of a local agent. As gently and as diplomatically as possible I told him I did not think much of this, and then wrote a stiffish letter to the agent, explaining that I had agreed privately with the owner to buy the boat, and had been mucked about by him for too long. I told them the price I was prepared to pay, which was the figure previously agreed (less of course the extra £100), and said I wanted a decision, a straight 'yes' or 'no' within 48 hours. If it was to be 'yes', then I wanted to take the boat away within seven days.

This produced an immediate reaction from the agent, who was on the phone within a couple of hours. He said the owner wanted more money, so patiently I explained that I was not negotiating, and asked him to read my letter again. The 'yes' came back within an hour, and this time was subsequently confirmed in writing. With regard to the date of the handover, the day I had specified happened to be August Bank Holiday, which the agent said presented difficulties. I told him I could see no valid reason for not handing over on this day — nor for that matter on a Shrove Tuesday or Christmas Day if necessary — but if it was quite impossible to transact business on a Bank Holiday, then we could make it the following day.

So Pat and I found ourselves in the bar at the Royal Lymington Yacht Club where the ceremony was to take place. Pat had come from London and was there at the appointed hour, I had motored down from Cheshire, had been delayed, and was late. By the time I arrived the whisky had already begun to flow, and it was obvious that the owner, who was a very decent chap, sincerely regretted his previous behaviour and was trying hard to make amends. Pat told me later that he had also tried to persuade her to crew for him in the new boat he was buying, so perhaps it was as well I arrived when I did!

Differences, however, were soon forgotten, and we had a friendly and jolly meeting, the net result of which was that it went on far too long and we missed our tide up the Solent. We were planning to spend the night in Cowes, and take *Peradventure* over to Bucklers Hard in the Beaulieu River the following day, where Marine Services had a temporary mooring for us, and to do this comfortably we needed about two and a half hours of fair tide, the wind being very light sou-westerly. But instead of leaving Lymington at 15.00 hours (HW Portsmouth being at 16.45) it was nearer 17.00 before we managed to tear ourselves away from our new-found friends. If we had had more sense, and rather less whisky, we would have stayed the night in Lymington, but having waited so long for *Peradventure* we were both desperate to get to sea.

The gentle sail down the Lymington River was delightful and relaxing, and as the buoys slipped slowly by, the knowledge that at last we were afloat again in our own little ship gradually stole over us, and all the frustrations and irritations of the past few months disappeared into our softly gurgling wake. The sky was overcast and the breeze was fitful but we sat there revelling in our surroundings, gazing at the marshes on either side and the hundreds of yachts on their moorings, and waving to the passengers on the Yarmouth Ferry as we threaded our way down the river. The Isle of Wight loomed up ahead: from nowhere does the island look more romantic and mysterious than from the entrance to the Lymington River.

It was a full hour before Jack-in-the-Basket was abeam and we were able to turn up the Solent. The ebb had already begun to run, though being a neap tide it was not very strong, and in my euphoric state, brought about by the twin intoxicants of water and whisky, I sat at the tiller dreaming away, not realizing that we were making very little progress. As the ebb strengthened so the wind died, and after battling for some time and getting nowhere we just had to start the engine. At 18.35 the sun set and it became appreciably colder, and as the light gradually faded it became obvious that with a foul tide for several more hours we were in for a long haul up to Cowes.

The decision I then took was a faulty one. With hindsight, and a clear head, it would have been better to have given in and run back either to Lymington or across to Yarmouth, but as we were now approaching Hamstead Ledge I decided to put into Newtown. Now, the Newtown entrance is easy enough in daylight, although you have to be careful for the channel is narrow and there are extensive mud flats on either hand. But it is another matter entirely in the dark, for there are no lights to guide you and no outstanding features in the landscape, in fact it is not until you are very close in that the opening into the harbour becomes apparent.

As we approached the entrance I had certain misgivings, for the buoy we were looking for is very small and inconspicuous, and there was a strong athwartships tide. The sea was not really rough, but there was certainly a bit of a popple, and this did not make life any easier. I knew the tide was setting us strongly to starboard, and tried to allow for this by steering to port, but in the event did not allow enough, and we came to a rather bumpy halt on the shingle bank to starboard. It was quite dark by now, and though there was no immediate danger it was irritating to have put our new ship aground on our first cruise, and on a falling tide. Pat was very forbearing about this, though the bumping was rather unpleasant, fortunately it sounded worse than it really was.

A few casts with the lead from the dinghy showed where the deeper water was and I ran out the kedge into the channel so that we could pull her off as soon as she floated, but it was a rather gloomy thought that it would not be low water till about 23.00, and we might have to wait for another couple of hours after that before she floated. In the meantime there was nothing we could do except try and be patient, so Pat cooked us a meal, which we ate in a rather depressed silence.

In the hours that followed Pat managed to get some sleep, and I had plenty of time to ponder on the foolishness of trying to enter, in the dark, a narrow and unlit channel that I had only ever navigated once before, and in broad daylight at that. The time passed very slowly, there was no moon, and though the shoreline could be dimly seen it was impossible to judge how far away it was. Several miles away to the north, on the other side of the Solent, a few twinkling lights were visible, but these could have been in another world. A chill little breeze got up and it was pretty lonely out there in the dark with *Peradventure* gently rocking to and fro but with her keel held fast.

As the tide rose she started to bump again, and I kept a gentle strain on the anchor warp so that each time she lifted she would edge a few inches towards the deeper water and freedom. It was a wonderful moment when the warp went limp in my hands and I realized she had finally slipped off the bank and was back afloat. We lost no time in starting the engine, recovering the anchor, and heading away from the land. The time was just after midnight.

Giving her a good offing we turned to the north-east, and with a fair tide under us went romping up the Solent towards Egypt Point. There was quite a sea running by now and the spray that was thrown up by her bow as she put her head down into the waves caught the light from the

navigation lamps, so that we had a red curtain to port and a green one to starboard.

Just before we reached Gurnard a cargo steamer of about 10,000 tons passed us, outward bound. Her bridge was in darkness, but her port navigation light glowed bright red, and lights could be seen in the crews' quarters aft. She was travelling quite slowly, but pushing a great wedge of water before her, and her wash, which we could see coming towards us in the darkness, was tremendous. When she had passed, the dull thump of her engines persisted for some time, gradually fading out as she disappeared down the Solent towards the Needles and the open sea.

The exhilaration of being under way again, the sights and sounds of the sea, the various buoys winking away in the darkness, and the constant rushing of the water against *Peradventure*'s hull, soon revived our flagging spirits, and the hour it took us to reach the mouth of the Medina River passed all too quickly. As we slid into the quiet and calm waters of Cowes Harbour, and passed smoothly through the sleeping town, I reflected on how easy it was when sailing to make mistakes, and how a moment of carelessness could endanger your ship and even the lives of those aboard, and I made a silent vow to be more careful in the future. I don't think I ever put *Peradventure* on the mud again.

16

Captain O.M. Watts

If you're going to the Boat Show,
If your interest is in yachts,
If you want to look at fittings,
Or to buy a book on knots,
If your crew's demanding clothing,
Or your dashes need some dots,
Then for these, and all requirements
Come to Watts, Watts, Watts, Watts, Watts.

Thus ran an advertisement I wrote in the yachting press in the mid 1960s advertising the services to be obtained from Captain O.M. Watts Ltd, 'the Yacht Chandler and Agent, of Albemarle Street, London. W1.'

The late Captain O.M. Watts was a character, well known in yachting circles throughout the entire world. Indeed it is doubtful whether any other man knew so many yachting personalities, or had such an influence on the development of the sport in this country. And not only in this country either, for in whatever part of the world men sailed small boats, the name 'Captain O.M. Watts' was a household word.

After a career in the Merchant Navy Captain Watts left the sea in 1927 and founded the firm that made his name famous. 'Captain O.M. Watts Ltd' became by far the most famous yacht chandlers ever known, trading throughout the civilized world. The mail he received each morning was truly international in character, and his showroom in Albemarle Street just off Piccadilly became the meeting place for thousands of people from the most humble yachtsman to the aristocracy and even princes and kings.

But Ossie Watts was far more than just a yacht chandler. Soon after leaving the Merchant Service he became the instigator and first editor of *Reed's Nautical Almanac*, and his association with this publication continued without a break for fifty years. Before the war of 1939 he founded the Watts Sea School for the purpose of training young people

in the arts of navigation and seamanship, the theoretical instruction being carried out at Albemarle Street, with practical training at the weekends aboard his 54-ft MFV *South Star* in the Beaulieu River. He was justifiably proud of the fact that over a hundred of his students took boats to Dunkirk in 1940.

He was also involved in yacht design, both on his own account and with other designers, and it was his initiative that brought into being the famous 'Z' 4-tonner designed by Dr Harrison Butler. Charts too were an interest of his, and the well known Stanford's Charts for Yachtsmen were prepared under his supervision.

All in all, his interests in the yachting world were legion, and his energy and dedication unbounded. He worked every day of the week from early in the morning to late in the evening, and his business premises in Albemarle Street were a hive of activity. Though some called his methods old fashioned — he would not have a typewriter in the place, for example — his attention to detail was extraordinary. Every single order had his personal attention, and though his insistence on being involved in everything, and his inability to delegate responsibility, sometimes drove his staff to the verge of distraction, his personality shone through it all, and in a rather miraculous way his organization, or the lack of it, somehow triumphed and the business was hugely successful.

Pat Withams was eighteen years old when she went to work for Captain Watts, and she stayed with him for thirteen years, becoming a loyal and trusted assistant. She was already a keen and experienced sailor, having crewed in both *Merlin* and *Grayling*, as well as owning her own boat, and it was through her influence that my son Anthony, when he left his job as mate of a Thames Sailing Barge, was taken on temporarily, pending his call-up for National Service. In the event he was never called up, but stayed on for a time to run the packing department.

It was also through Pat's influence that I too became involved in the organization, and that Anthony and I were both invited to weekends aboard *South Star*, where we spent many happy hours sampling the delights of 'big ship' sailing. Perhaps one of the longest trips we did was to Folkestone where we were due to act as safety boat on a cross-channel dinghy race to Boulogne. The weather was not too kind for this event and there were several capsizes in mid-channel which we had to sort out, but my principal recollections of the event were two in number.

Firstly there was the suppressed hilarity caused in the wheelhouse when Captain Watts was trying out a new shortwave radio with which he tried to call up the Varne Lightship. He sat cross-legged on the floor of the wheelhouse cuddling this instrument and started calling '*South Star* calling Varne Light Vessel. *South Star* calling Varne Light Vessel.' But after a period of nil response, and with growing frustration and irritability, he started calling 'South Varne calling Star Light Vessel' and various other permutations. He never did make contact with them, although we passed within half a mile of the lightship.

The second memory concerns our entry into Boulogne. As we approached the harbour he suddenly asked me if I would like to take her in, and I must confess that my bosom swelled with pride at being trusted with what was, to me, a large ship. When we were well inside the harbour Captain Watts was quite unable to decide where to moor up, and it was not until we reached the top of the harbour and began to run out of water that a decision was forced upon him. Later I discovered that he had never been into Boulogne before, and this was the real reason why he had entrusted his ship to me.

Another occasion was when Anthony and I sailed with him from Beaulieu to Cowes. Halfway down the river we ran into a bank of fog and he became very worried, running round the deck gazing into the fog on all sides and wondering what to do. Finally he decided to turn back. Anthony was on the wheel at the time and with the confidence of youth he swung the ship round and we were soon back in the sunshine. The Skipper then decided to have another go and this time we made it, but at great cost to his nerves. My recollection of this incident is of catching Anthony's eye at the height of the indecision and seeing him raise his eyebrows and shrug his shoulders as much as to say 'What *is* all the fuss about?'

However, these little displays of nervousness were not important, and did not detract in any way from the fact that Captain Watts was extremely knowledgeable in all aspects of boat handling, and was a most generous and large-hearted man who liked nothing better than sharing his pleasures with others. He was a great character, and a good friend.

My own involvement in his business was somewhat spasmodic but fascinating for I was able to do a number of surveys for him on various types of boat and also several boat deliveries. The latter were always interesting, for one never knew the type of boat that would turn up next. One I particularly remember is *Dormy*, that belonged to a friend of Captain Watts who wanted someone to help him sail her from Falmouth to Cowes.

Dormy was a motor boat of about 20 ft overall length, and not really the sort of boat in which to go tearing about the Channel in English weather. Basically she was an open boat, but I was assured that she had a small cabin up forward, so that living aboard was possible if not actually comfortable. But her great attraction was her engine. This occupied the greater part of the vessel and was a Gardner diesel, a huge beast whose horsepower I have since forgotten but which was big enough for a boat twice the size of *Dormy*. The boat herself had been built by Moody to the owner's own specification, of good materials, and was certainly well-found. He had intended to use her for fishing, which explained the enormous cockpit, in the centre of which, in a large box, crouched the Gardner.

I first met the owner in a first class compartment of a train at Paddington Station, and we travelled down to Falmouth together. He was a large man, with a cultured accent, and well provided for, and we chatted happily about boats for a time, until he fell asleep. My brief, I had a been told, was to skipper the boat and to be responsible for the navigation, about which the owner knew nothing, but in the event it turned out that I was also expected to be ship's cook. Fortunately his tastes in food were simple and bordered on the frugal, and he did not expect any serious cooking. He was adamant on one point only, he would not permit a frying pan aboard.

As I got to know him better I found him to be a man of civilized tastes, and easy to get on with. Obviously he had plenty of money and was generous in its use without being ostentatious. He had one favourite expression which he used frequently, but which was capable of such a variation in tone and meaning that it never became boring. This was 'Ho! Ho!', and he could get such a wealth of meaning into this and such a variety of emphasis, that he reminded me of Dr Chasuble in *The Importance of Being Earnest* who claimed of his sermon on the meaning of the manna in the wilderness that it could be adapted for any occasion, be it joyful or distressing.

We were booked into the Falmouth Hotel for the night with the intention of being off the following morning, but at this point the weather broke, and for three days it was inadvisable, if not impossible, to leave the harbour. The gale was sou'westerly and we could see that a horrendous sea had built up outside. But these three days were not wasted. *Dormy* was on a mooring and I borrowed a dinghy each morning and went out to her, familiarizing myself with her and with her engine. One morning we went for a trip across the harbour to St Mawes and met some pretty rough seas, which satisfied me that she was a good sea boat, capable of dealing with all we expected or intended to meet. For the rest of the time we met a charming couple staying in the hotel with their two children and spent several hours happily playing table tennis with them in the hotel's games room.

On the fourth day we were able to leave. It was still rough but we had wasted so much time that we were both anxious to be on our way. Also I was beginning to be worried that I would not be able to complete the trip without a break, for in a few days time I had a commitment back in Kent that I was unable to cancel. The owner was very reasonable about this problem, time being of no importance to him, and he was quite willing for me to leave him in some harbour on the way while I dashed up to Kent and back. So we went on our way without any pressure, which is the right way to enjoy sailing.

Dormy behaved well at sea but close to the land the backwash from the cliffs caused a very confused sea and it was not until we stood off for about two miles that things quietened down a bit and the wave pattern became more regular. The weather was not too pleasant and it rained most of the time, and within a few hours we were discussing where we should spend the night. The owner favoured Plymouth, but as we approached the Sound we were met by a disgusting mass of flotsam, household refuse, cardboard cartons, rotten fruit, etc, and I was able to persuade him that it was better to go on a little further.

There was an ulterior motive in this, as I very much wanted to go into Newton Ferrers on the River Yealm. Apart from the fact that this is one of the most beautiful little harbours on the South Coast, I believe that at one time it had the distinction of having a woman as Harbour Master, and this woman was none other than Miss Agnes Russell, sister of Pat Russell of Hythe who was the owner of *Ardglass* and a friend of Captain Watts. Ossie used to tell a delightful story about Miss Russell, who was a very capable woman and what the French would describe as '*formidable*'. One day in conversation with her he suggested facetiously that perhaps she should be called the Harbour Mistress. She fixed him with a stern and forbidding eye. 'Harbour *Master*, if you please Captain Watts. I would have you know that I am no one's mistress!'

As we approached the land aboard *Dormy* the owner expressed some scepticism as to my ability to negotiate the slightly tricky entrance to the River Yealm, for until you are quite close in no entrance can be seen, but I assured him that things would be alright, and in we went. Newton Ferrers really is the most delightful spot with high wooded banks coming down to the waters edge. Here and there among the trees are pretty houses, though not so many as to detract from the utter peace and quietness of the river.

The owner announced his intention of staying aboard through the evening, but I wanted to go ashore and explore, so when the Harbour Master (a man) was helping us to find a mooring I asked him if he could lend me a dinghy. This was readily forthcoming, and in the event we both went ashore and had quite a pleasant walk, finishing up with a drink in the local hotel. As we settled down for the night, watching the lights in the houses going out one by one, I was convinced that this was the most peaceful spot on earth, and even my companion agreed that it was preferable to Plymouth.

The following morning it was still blowing quite hard when we left, and raining intermittently, and though we had the east-going tide under us a lot of spray came aboard and we got pretty wet. Our first target was Bolt Head, to the west of Salcombe, and I aimed to pass this with an offing of at least a mile, as all these headlands have their patches of rough water close in. Immediately after Salcombe we had Prawle Point and then Start Point to round.

Off Prawle Point we passed a lone yachtsman in a 25 ft sloop, and exchanged a cheery greeting with him as he was shaping up to enter Salcombe. The following day in Dartmouth we were stunned to hear everyone talking about a single-handed yachtsman who had been wrecked and drowned on Salcombe Bar, just about the time we had seen this sloop. The sailing directions for Salcombe say that the bar is dangerous in strong on-shore winds and should not be attempted when wind is against tide, but it seemed impossible to believe that so soon after we had spoken to this man he had met such a violent end.

For centuries Start Point has been a well known landmark to sailors passing up Channel, and it was certainly a milestone on our little voyage. As we rounded it and altered course to the north east the sun suddenly came out and the sea started to moderate. It had been agreed that we would enter Dartmouth and that I would leave *Dormy* there while I went to Kent, but it was a couple of hours from the Start before we were in and had found a suitable mooring. By this time the wind and blazing sunshine had played havoc with my salt-encrusted face, and I was suffering from a bad attack of sun and salt burn. As soon as possible I went ashore to a chemist, and I can still remember the expression on the face of the middle-aged lady pharmacist who took one look at me and exclaimed 'Oh, you naughty man!' She gave me some lotion, but it was too late, and my nose blew up into a blister almost twice its size.

By the time I returned to Dartmouth my face had returned almost to normal. *Dormy* and her owner were still where I had left them and I don't think he had even been ashore. I had left him plenty of food including several tins of grapefruit segments, which incidentally he swore he had never come across before, and to which he had rapidly become addicted. While I was away I think he lived mainly on these and cups of coffee.

The next stage of the voyage was plain sailing, on a compass course direct to Portland Bill. We passed inside the race and made for Weymouth where for the first time we were moored on a trot with other boats. We dined ashore and in the morning set off on the last leg of the trip, the twenty miles or so to Cowes.

Coming through Hurst narrows we met as big a swell as we had experienced anywhere, but we were soon through it and shooting up the Solent past Yarmouth. In Cowes we picked up a mooring off the Groves and Gutteridge Yard, and suddenly it all seemed the most dreadful anti-climax. Why does it ever have to end? As we waited silently for the taxi that was to take us to the Ferry the owner suddenly looked at me and smiled. 'Ho! Ho!' he said. I think he had enjoyed it.

★ ★ ★

The vital statistics of a boat are almost as important as the vital statistics of a woman, indeed they are perhaps more important for they tell you not only what she is like to look at, but also tell you how she will behave. And this is of great interest if by any chance you have to take her to sea. One of the most revealing of statistics (in a boat) is the ratio of beam to overall length, for the lower this is the more tendency the boat will have to roll in a seaway, and the more unpleasant you will find her company. Modern boats tend to be chubbier than old ones, and nowadays any craft with a beam less than a third the overall length is regarded with a certain amount of horror.

So that when Captain Watts asked me to deliver the motor yacht *Orthia* to France from her mooring in Rochester I looked with lacklustre eye at her vital statistics, for her overall length was 47 ft 6 in and her beam 10 ft 1 in. Truly a narrow-gutted beast.

Orthia had been built in Chester in 1915 so she was already fifty years old when I met her in the 1960s, and she had seen better as well as younger days. But there was no doubt that she had once been beautiful and gracious, and it was possible to believe that during her lifetime many men had loved her. But now she was to be sold away to a French owner in Calais, and someone had to be found to take her across the Channel where her new owner was enthusiastically waiting to restore her to her former beauty.

It was the beginning of March and there had been a heavy fall of snow. It was very cold. Anthony, who was always ready to chance his arm where a boat was concerned, agreed to come with me, and we reckoned to take a couple of days over the trip with a stop in Ramsgate which was approximately half way. Starting the two engines was fun, for the electrical wiring was in very poor shape and when you switched on in the engine room there were minor firework displays, with sparks running along some of the wires. An idiosyncracy of the system was that having started one engine you had then to reverse the battery leads before being able to start the other. But once started they ran pretty well, and we thundered along at a speed of at least 8 or 9 knots.

The journey to Ramsgate was cold but otherwise uneventful, and we stayed in the outer harbour for the night as we wished to be off very early in the morning to catch the south going tide. We were up well before dawn, quite prepared for a couple of hours sailing in the dark, but were a bit shocked to find it extremely foggy as well. Everything was very still and rather eerie in the harbour, and the fog was so thick that we only dimly saw the pierheads as we slipped between them. And then we were swallowed up in the fog and were on our own.

Sailing in fog is always a pretty weird experience, and when it is dark as well you need a considerable amount of faith to keep plugging on with only the dimly lighted compass card to guide you. It is very easy to imagine objects looming up ahead and to start querying the accuracy of the compass. We were proceeding due south from Ramsgate. On our starboard hand was the coast of Kent, and to port the dreaded Goodwin Sands. It was very important that we should not hit either of these and equally vital to the safety of all concerned that we should not meet some other vessel on a reciprocal course. But there was no sound other than the noise of our own engines, and we pressed on, keeping our fingers crossed.

As dawn broke the fog began to thin a little, and soon we were relieved to pick up the sound of the fog signal from the South Goodwin Light Vessel, a diaphone blowing twice every minute. This sound was on our port bow and told us we were on course and well clear of trouble. As the light strengthened so the visibility improved until suddenly there was the South Goodwin on our port beam about a mile and a half away, the only ship in sight. The sky was grey, the sea was grey, but it was calm, and we only had another twenty miles to go. Thankfully we had breakfast and felt considerably more cheerful.

In Calais we were directed into the yacht basin where we had been several times before in *Merlin* and in *Grayling*, and moored up alongside the wall. We were in plenty of time for Anthony to catch the ferry back to Dover — there was no point in us both staying on to hand over *Orthia* to the port authorities — and after seeing him off I tidied up the ship, and then set off to find the man I had to contact.

This last phase of the operation then became almost surrealist, and I began to wonder whether I had not strayed into one of those French films where slightly improbable events take place in completely improbable places. It had been arranged that I should be given a receipt for the boat and paid the delivery fee which, if I remember correctly, was 1500 francs, and had expected this transaction to be conducted in an office. But no. After several enquiries I was directed to a corrugated iron shed in the dock area where I found the man I had to see.

He was dressed in blue overalls and wore the inevitable beret, and he was sitting at a plain kitchen type table on which stood a half empty bottle of wine. The only other furniture in the room consisted of a cupboard, another chair, a large coke-burning stove, and a bicycle. But he was expecting me and we got on well together, though our conversation was necessarily limited as the French he spoke was foreign to my ears, and the French I spoke was equally foreign to his.

I handed over *Orthia*'s papers and he painstakingly wrote out a rather crude receipt, then opened a drawer in the table and took out a great wadge of dirty notes and carefully counted out 1500 francs which he handed me with a slight bow, and for which I gave him a receipt. Then we stood up, shook hands, said '*bon jour*', and I left him.

The next ferry to Dover did not keep me waiting very long. The bar was warm and comfortable and, my goodness, did I enjoy that gin and tonic! And that, I thought, was that. *Orthia* was safely delivered, I had been paid, all the loose ends had been tied up.

But there was a sequel, and this took me back into the make-belief world of films again. Soon after I arrived home the telephone range and a man's voice said:

'This is the Dover CID. I understand you were in Ramsgate Harbour yesterday in a yacht called *Orthia* and left before dawn for France.'

I agreed that this was so.

'A large quantity of cigarettes was stolen in Ramsgate during the night, and we wondered if you knew anything about it.'

I had to laugh at the implication.

'Surely you don't think I have been trying to flog English cigarettes in France?'

'No, no' he said, 'We just wondered if you had seen anything suspicious in the early hours of the morning.'

I would have loved to have been able to help him, to have told him of shadowy figures on the quayside, of a lorry with its engine running, but with no lights, but alas I was a disappointing witness. We had seen nothing and heard nothing, and regretfully I had to leave him to seek his information elsewhere.

Delivering and surveying yachts were all part of the help we tried to give to Captain Watts' brokerage department which had a long list of yachts for sale. For some time I wrote his advertisements for the yachting press, and Anthony illustrated them with delightful little pen and ink drawings of the boats concerned.

Another idea we tried in advertising — with the object of attracting attention — was a series of advertisements in verse. These were supposed to be humorous and each one was headed 'A Watticism', and I like to think they achieved their object. They certainly attracted attention and comment, though Ossie was not quite sure whether he approved, for his pals in the City Livery Yacht Club used to pull his leg about them. A typical example, taken from *Motor Boat and Yachting* is shown below, and another is given at the head of this chapter.

"A WATTICISM"

. . . . truck

. . . . cranse

In the street of a thousand meters,
At the sign of the swinging ship,
There's a shop of delectable yacht goods,
A shop that is well worth a trip.

We can furnish your ship from her keelson,
To the truck of her highest top-mast,
We can kit you out too if you wish, sir,
With clothes that are smart and will last.

There is everything here for the yachtsman,
And nothing your ship, sir, need lack,
From the cranse on the end of the bowsprit,
To the tirpswob (or bowsprit spelt back).

And if you do not own a boat, sir,
Please do not despair of your lot,
You have only to drop us a postcard,
And we'll sell you a very fine yacht.

. . . . . . tirpswob

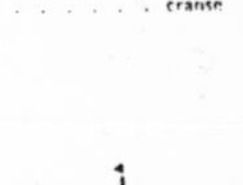

. . . . a very fine yacht

"WATTS FOR YACHTS"

CAPTAIN O. M. WATTS LTD

49 ALBEMARLE STREET, PICCADILLY, LONDON, W.1

Telephone: HYDe Park 4633 Telegrams: 'Yachtnavi, London, W.1'

Our introduction to the Solent area through excursions in *South Star* was a new and fascinating experience, for though I knew Southampton Water and Spithead well enough from the days when I was an engineer in the *Queen Mary* — days which I wrote about in the book *Queen Mary: Her early years recalled* — I had never sailed these waters in small boats. So it was to dear old Ossie Watts and *South Star* that we owed the change in habitat that was to have such a lasting effect on our lives, and ultimately led us to come and live in the Isle of Wight.

PART 4

NARIJA

It's the wave of the sea in my blood, and I'll never be free,
Never be free all my days from the sea's wild crying,
The crash of the waves on the rocks and the far-flung spray,
The windy call of the gulls and the spume-flakes flying.

TERESA HOOLEY

17

Yarmouth and the South Coast

THE autumn gales arrived a little early in 1974 and caught Pat and I in the middle of a late holiday in *Peradventure*. We had only reached Yarmouth and for four days the sou-westerly winds blew a whole gale and we were unable to go any further. Outside, the conditions were fearful, but in this charming little harbour we were as snug as could be. Yarmouth is an interesting spot in which to be gale-bound, and the George Hotel had long been a favourite of ours, so that the evenings passed very pleasantly.

During the day time we rowed round the harbour looking at the boats, and it was there that we first saw the motor yacht *Narija*. We had no intention whatsoever of changing boats, and our interest was purely perfunctory, but all boats are fascinating, and particularly those that have a touch of class. And *Narija* certainly had that. She was obviously a thoroughbred, and equally obviously had seen better days. She was moored in the shabbier part of the harbour, between two ugly boats, which prevented us getting a good look at her, and she had a 'For Sale' notice in her wheelhouse. But after commenting that she looked a nice boat, we rowed on.

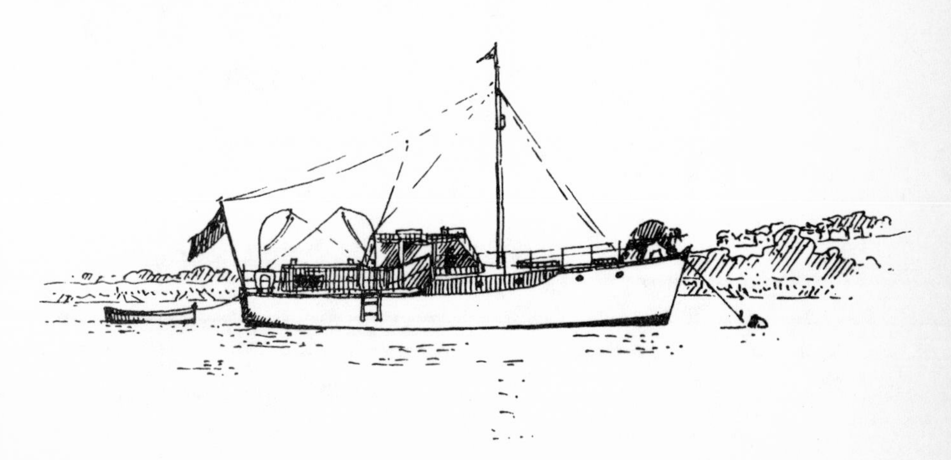

But the next day as we rowed round in the dinghy we passed her again and Pat suddenly said 'Let's go aboard and have a look at her', so we tied up the dinghy, clambered over the fishing boat next to her and climbed aboard. It was then we realized what a beauty she was — or had been — and were able to hazard a guess as to her pedigree.

Narija had been designed by John Bain and built by James A. Silver at Rosneath, and every inch of her was pleasing. She had wide laid decks, a most gratifying sheer, and her large wheelhouse was set well aft and let into the deck, this being a typical John Bain feature and usually the sign of a sturdy and sea-kindly vessel. We peered through the wheelhouse windows and our interest quickened; she was truly a little ship.

Over dinner that night we talked about her, still without the slightest intention of buying her, for we were very satisfied with, and fond of, our present boat *Peradventure*, who was also a thoroughbred. But we had on several occasions talked about my impending retirement in a couple of years time, and agreed that sooner or later we should probably want to give up sail and move to power. We were also in agreement that when we did, a boat like *Narija* would be ideal, either for local and Channel cruising, or for going further afield.

Inevitably, we called on the local yacht agency next morning and enquired about her. Yes, we were told, she was for sale and at a very reasonable price as her owner had been unable to keep her up and she was in a very shabby condition. Particulars of *Narija* were produced, from which we learned that she was built in 1946, entirely of teak, and her vital statistics were LOA 36 ft, Beam 10 ft 4 in, and Draft 3 ft 3 in.

Now, 1946 was not a very good year for building a wooden boat in Britain where after seven years of war good timber was hard to find, but teak was an entirely different matter for with teak you could relax, secure in the knowledge that there would be no rot aboard. However, the most exciting particular was that she had been re-engined in 1973, only twelve months previously, and her two Mercedes-Benz 36/42 diesels were as yet barely run in.

A young lady from the agency accompanied us aboard, and the next couple of hours were among the most interesting, yet curious, we had ever spent in looking at a boat. Her accommodation was straightforward, conventional, and old-fashioned. Up forward in the forecastle was a toilet compartment containing a loo and the biggest white wash hand basin I had ever seen in a 36 ft boat. There was plenty of light, with portholes port and starboard, and a fixed iron ladder up to the fore hatch. There was standing headroom, and had the washbasin been half the size the compartment would have been twice as comfortable.

A central door led into the saloon — a good solid teak door that closed with a satisfying click — but the saloon was perhaps the most disappointing part of the ship. The basic cabin layout was conventional, with two large settee berths, one on each side of a central table, and the squabs lifted up to form two more bunk beds. There were plenty of shelves and lockers, and the finish and workmanship of the woodwork was excellent, but we felt that a more modern layout would have made better use of the space available.

Aft of the saloon on the port side was the galley, very well fitted out with calor gas cooker and fridge, stainless steel sink, etc, and on the starboard side a navigating table with drawers and lockers under, a large two-way radio and a switchboard and fuse box.

Up a few steps from this compartment was the large square wheelhouse with sliding doors port and starboard on to the side decks, and a very good clear view all the way round. The engine room was below the wheelhouse and the twin Morse controls were mounted alongside the wheel, the helmsman being provided with a very comfortable chair.

Aft of the wheelhouse was the owner's cabin, delightfully fitted out with two single berths, a dressing table, hanging wardrobe to port, and a small but well-equipped toilet compartment to starboard. At the after end of this cabin was a hatchway to the after deck.

On deck and forward of the wheelhouse the space seemed enormous, and there was ample room on the side and after decks. Davits were fitted on the port side aft and the dinghy was stowed on chocks on the after coach roof. Altogether a very satisfactory and seamanlike layout, and we were suitably impressed.

We spent a considerable time rummaging about, had all the carpets up to look in the bilges, and explored the engine room, which besides the two new and gleaming Mercedes Benz diesels had a small charging engine. There were two fuel tanks, port and starboard, each holding 34 gallons, and ample water storage capacity.

But the curious, and slightly pathetic, part of our first visit to *Narija* was in the accommodation. The yacht agent had described her as being in 'end of season' condition, and we soon discovered that this was a considerable understatement. It is true that her topsides and hull were not in too bad shape though sorely in need of a lick of paint, and her laid decks urgently required attention, but down below she was filthy. Never had we seen a more deplorable case of neglect in a beautiful little ship.

In the galley was a flip-top rubbish bin full and overflowing, and there was rubbish everywhere. Empty cigarette and cigar packets and full ashtrays were all over the place, and every locker and drawer contained an empty whisky bottle. There were packs of cards everywhere, and the pathetic story all these items told was only too plain to see. The young lady from the agency apologized for the state the boat was in, and commented on the number of playing cards about. She expressed an interest in the game of Patience, and before we knew where we were we found ourselves teaching her the three variations of the game that we ourselves occasionally played.

So the first afternoon we spent aboard *Narija* was a rather strange one, but it served to increase our interest in her and led to conversations with the yacht agency, the result of which was an agreement to buy her, subject to survey and to something being done about the decks, and providing that a reasonable price could be obtained for *Peradventure.*

Events then happened in quick succession. *Peradvenutre* sold very quickly, and the survey on *Narija* was reassuring, the only major work needed being the re-caulking of the decks. We took her out to sea and were delighted with the way she handled. This was our first experience of twin engines, and the ability to move the boat in any direction, and even to spin her on her own axis, was novel and intriguing, and was an asset we found extremely useful on more than one occasion in the future when manoeuvring her in small and busy harbours.

The other great benefit was the additional space both on deck and down below. After a 7-ton sailing boat, comfortable though she was, *Narija* at 14 tons Thames Measurement felt like an ocean liner, and we revelled in the simple pleasure of being able to walk about freely on deck without tripping over sheets and their fairleads. We soon agreed that our change from sail to power had been a good move, and began to look forward to our first cruise.

★ ★ ★

The collaboration between John Bain the designer and Messrs. James A Silver of Rosneath, the builder, lasted for many years and resulted in over 100 quality yachts being built. Most of these were in the range from 10-20 tons TM, but there were many others, from 6 tons up to 78 tons, and it is true to say that they were all thoroughbreds, John Bain's designs being immediately recognizable for their beauty of line, and Silver's workmanship having built up an enviable reputation.

Their traditional hull shape ensured that all John Bain's boats were sea-kindly, and gave as comfortable a ride as possible, but they were by no means fast, and some people have criticized them for this. The modern trend is to put emphasis on speed, and indeed a friend commented that

Narija would be no use to him as he liked to be able to leave the Solent after breakfast and be in Cherbourg for lunch. Fortunately, being used to sailing boats, and to working our tides, speed did not worry us and we were quite happy to trundle along at about 8 knots.

Narija with her new Mercedes engines would of course go faster than this, but only at the expense of considerably higher fuel consumption, and we found from experience that at 1500 rpm each engine would burn about half a gallon per hour, but would only give her about 6 knots. At 2500 rpm her speed would be increased to 9 knots, but fuel consumption was doubled, so that normally we kept our engine revs at between 2000 and 2500. The new engines had cost the previous owner a lot of money and he had fitted them because he was disappointed with her speed, but he had ignored the fact that her hull shape was such that 9 or 10 knots was really as much as could be expected. (On the subject of fuel consumption it is perhaps worth recording that diesel fuel at this time cost 29p per gallon.)

The manoeuvrability of *Narija* with her twin engines never ceased to delight me, and this was demonstrated very clearly at the start of our first major cruise, when we decided to visit some of our old sailing haunts up the east coast, and follow this by spending the winter in St Katherine's Dock in London. The first phase of this trip was to take *Narija* from Yarmouth across to Buckler's Hard where we were going to fuel her and also pick up our crew, and on this first leg we were accompanied by a friend and business colleague of mine, Peter Cornish. Peter and I had been spending a couple of days in Southampton on business, and when this was over we crossed to the island and met Pat aboard *Narija* in Harold Hayles Boatyard.

She was moored just below Yarmouth Bridge in the middle of a tight cluster of other boats, and there was very little room to manoeuvre, but the ease with which she was extricated from this position was remarkable. It was made possible by the fact that the engines were controlled by means of Morse combined throttle and gear controls, and by manipulating these — without touching the wheel — she came out of her very tight hole, turned, and threaded her way between other boats, with no trouble at all. Pat and Peter stood by with fenders in case of need, but actually these were not required, and we were soon nosing our way out of the harbour and into the Solent.

At Buckler's Hard we filled both tanks up with fuel, and topped up the water tanks which held 200 gallons, and by the time our crew arrived we were ready for an early departure the following morning.

The two members of the crew were old and trusted friends. One was my son Anthony, whose experience of coastwise sailing in all sorts of boats now spanned, incredibly, a period of 25 years, and the other was a very distinguished deep-water sailor, Adrian Seligman. Adrian's experience of the sea was vast. As a very young man he had sailed in wind jammers, and while still in his 20's had bought a barquentine, assembled a crew, and sailed round the world. His subsequent book, *The Voyage of the Cap Pilar* has been a sailing classic ever since its publication in 1939. Like all truly great men Adrian is modest and unassuming, and it was a very great honour to have him aboard.

We were off at 06.30 the following morning on the next leg of our voyage, which was to take us from Buckler's Hard to Dover. The sky was overcast but the clouds were high and there was every prospect of a pleasant and peaceful day. What breeze there was came from the north-west, and was only about force 2. We left five hours before high water Dover, for this would give us the benefit of several hours of east going tide, and we romped down the river in the early morning peace and quiet after a rather sketchy first breakfast.

Outside, the sea was calm, and once past Ryde we shaped a course for the Owers Light Vessel, about twenty miles further on. There is something magical about clearing the land and seeing nothing but sea ahead of you, and even on the simplest voyage there is a feeling of adventure and excitement. When, in addition, you are in your own boat, responsible for its conduct, and the lives of all those aboard, you realize just how lucky you are.

The Nab Tower to the south of us was abeam by 09.00, and the Owers just over an hour later. By this time the Isle of Wight had disappeared into the mist astern, and away to the north Selsey Bill was a faint blur.

Aboard *Narija* we were trying hard to get used to the difference between a motor yacht and a sailing boat. In *Peradventure* we would have been sitting out in the open air in the cockpit, with just enough room for the four of us, and with one of us cuddling the tiller and watching the compass and the burgee. The wind being light nor-westerly the boom would have been broad off to starboard, we would probably have been rolling a bit, and our speed through the water would have been perhaps three knots, and over the ground no more than 4½.

But in *Narija*'s wheelhouse it was quite different. We were protected all round from the weather, though in fact the sliding doors on either side were open. We all had cushioned seats to sit on, but could walk about on the carpeted floor when we felt like it, and the helmsman sat in a comfortable chair. In front of him was a row of instruments showing the revs for each engine, oil pressure and battery charging rate, etc. If he got tired of sitting he could stand up at the side of the wheel, and could easily consult the chart which was spread out nearby. If he let go of the wheel the boat did not suddenly change course, as happens in most sailing boats when the tiller is released.

Though there was of course a continual noise from the engines this was not loud enough to be unpleasant, and it was possible to carry on a normal conversation. Indeed, one of my happiest recollections of this particular trip was hearing Anthony and Adrian talking about boats, and swapping experiences.

But having said this, one has said it all, for the big difference is that in a motor vessel — providing the engines are running smoothly — there is absolutely nothing to do, and it can become terribly boring. In a sailing boat there are always minute adjustments that can be made to the sheets, and even to the halyards. There are sails to be changed, and one is always conscious of the wind, its strength and direction, and of being in control of a live thing. And of course it is very much more peaceful and exhilarating to be out in the open air, to be subjected to no mechanical noise, to have only the natural sounds of the wind and the sea, and the satisfying noise made by the boat as she ploughs through the water.

In retrospect it would seem that the principal activity aboard *Narija* as she proceeded steadily eastwards a few miles off the south coast of England was the preparation of food. We had a second breakfast of course, for the first one had been very early, coffee and biscuits were served as elevenses, and later we had a snack lunch. It was 10.10 when we passed the Owers and 14.00 when we reached our next mark, Beachy Head, and four hours is a long time when there is very little to do. Both engines were running sweetly at 2500 rpm, giving us about 9½ knots over the ground, so that we were making steady, if not spectacular, progress.

About seven miles past Beachy Head is the Royal Sovereign light vessel, or rather the huge Lanby Buoy that has replaced the lightship, and here a change in course was necessary. Adrian was navigating and came up with the new course, but said —

'By the way, if we don't change course, but stick to the old one, we can be in Boulogne in three hours!'

He had a twinkle in his eye as he said this, and I was not quite sure whether he was serious, but we did consider it before rejecting the suggestion as being, regrettably, impracticable.

Having changed course we now had another 24 miles to Dungeness, and the tide was turning against us so that our speed over the ground was considerably slower. It took us three hours to reach Dungeness and another two and a half hours before we arrived at Dover. The log records that we entered the harbour through the East Entrance at 20.30, and were anchored in the Camber and finished with engines by 20.45. Altogether we had been under way for 14¼ hours and had travelled about 120 miles, our average speed having been just under 8½ knots. The engines had behaved impeccably and had consumed 39 gallons of fuel, the consumption per engine thus being 1.4 gallons per hour. Engine speed throughout had been 2500 rpm.

It was a strange feeling being in Dover again, and being anchored in the Camber, which we had used so many times in *Merlin* and *Grayling*. The port was obviously busier, there being many newer and larger ferries bustling in and out, and one sensed that the welcome to visiting yachtsmen was a shade less enthusiastic than in the past. Continental ferries and small yachts are inevitably uneasy bedfellows, but the harbour authorities did not keep us standing off for very long before letting us in, and we were allowed to stay overnight in the Camber which is sheltered and quiet, apart from the characteristic cries from the seagulls that reverberate from the white cliffs.

In the morning we were off again early, our destination being Strood on the River Medway, where Anthony and Adrian were planning to leave us. As we did not have so far to go, and were not in a hurry, I kept the engine revs down to 2000, to measure the effect on fuel consumption and on speed, and in the event it did effect a saving in fuel without reducing our average speed appreciably.

Dover entrance, depart	06.55
South Foreland abeam	07.10
North Foreland abeam	09.50
Longnose Buoy abeam	10.10
West Last Buoy abeam	11.25
Garrison Point, Sheerness	13.25
Strood Pier	14.55

Total distance travelled in 8 hours = 66 miles, average speed being 8.25 knots. Fuel consumed 14½ gallons, or 0.9 gallons per hour per engine.

It is said to be inadvisable to re-visit places where one has been happy, for invariably one is disappointed, but Pat and I had been looking forward for some time to our return to the Medway and the east coast, and in many ways it was far from disappointing. At Strood the River Medway was still busy, though there were no Thames sailing barges about, and in the streets there seemed to be more traffic and noise. We had two weeks at our disposal before having to be in London, so we planned first to spend a few days relaxing in Stangate Creek lower down the Medway and then cross over to Essex to visit Brightlingsea before taking *Narija* up the Thames to St Katherine's Dock, where she was going to spend the winter.

Stangate was as delightful as ever, and for four days we lazed about, soaking up the sunshine, rowing up to Lower Halstow in the dinghy, marvelling at the sunsets and at the tranquility of the creek. Brightlingsea on the other hand had changed. Gone was the sleepy little fishing and sailing barge port, for it was now teeming with pleasure craft of all shapes and sizes, surf boarders, water skiers, sailing boats, motor boats, the lot. There was hardly a square inch of water left, and ashore it was no better. After spending an hour or two jostling with the crowds as we did our shopping, we quietly upped anchor and left, creeping slowly up Pyefleet Creek until we were well above the oyster beds. Here we found a spot miles away from anywhere, with just enough water to keep us afloat, and where there was no noise other than the cry of the birds, and occasionally a distant farm tractor.

When it was time to leave and return to civilization we both felt rejuvenated and able to face the world again. We had a leisurely fifty mile crossing of the Thames estuary back to Stangate Creek, and from there it was approximately another fifty miles to St Katherine's. The trip up London's river was interesting but depressing. I remembered the London docks from before the war when the river was full of life and shipping, and had not realized how much this had changed, and how completely this life had departed. On both sides of the river the docks were deserted and derelict, and yet the water was even more filthy than before and was full of flotsam and refuse. It was all very discouraging, and our morale was low as we sighed for the lost heaven of Pyefleet and Stangate.

We locked into St Katherine's at 13.25 and by 14.00 were berthed

alongside a pontoon in the East Basin. Our spirits began to rise, for the berth was very well found, with mains water and electricity and a toilet block with showers nearby. That evening we dined in the carvery at the Tower Hotel, and decided that life was not so bad after all.

18

Lead kindly light

ST KATHERINE'S Dock lies immediately downstream of the Tower of London and Tower Bridge, and was rescued from dereliction by a brave development which turned it into a haven for boats of many types, together with a complex of offices and flats in what had been warehouses. It was an up-market development, and our object in going there was to explore the possibilities of running our own small Public Relations and Publicity business there after my retirement. At the time office rents were reasonable, and the prospect of being able to keep *Narija* there as well was an additional incentive.

Unfortunately things did not work out as we had expected and we had to abandon the project, but *Narija* was in St Katherine's for nearly a year and during this period proved invaluable as a *pied-a-terre*. When we left, it was to bring her back to a permanent mooring in Yarmouth where we had bought a house.

The voyage back to the Isle of Wight divided itself up quite readily into four legs each of 50-60 miles, the first being from London to our favourite Medway anchorage in Stangate Creek, the second from Stangate

to Dover, the third from Dover to Newhaven, and the fourth from Newhaven to the Island.

We locked out of St Katherine's at 08.50 one June morning and proceeded to the nearby fuelling barge where we filled our tanks, and by 09.30 we had cast off and were heading down river. HW London Bridge was at 08.23 so that we had several hours of ebb under us, and in fact we had reached the Medway estuary by low water and took the first of the flood up into Stangate Creek, where we were anchored by 16.00. We had not hurried and had averaged, between St Katherine's and Sheerness, 8.3 knots.

The weather forecast for the next leg to Dover was wind variable force 2 becoming southerly 3-4, but when we set out at 07.30 the following morning there was no wind at all and it was foggy. However, it looked as though it might easily clear, and by the time we had groped our way down to Sheerness and out into the estuary the visibility was about half a mile. The sea was glassy calm, and in the mist it was difficult to see the division between sea and sky. In these conditions the light plays tricks and sometimes it is possible to see the next buoy as a little black speck far in the distance, while at others you appear to be almost on top of it when it looms up. But as we peered ahead we had no real difficulty in finding our string of buoys — the West Cant, the Spile, West Last, East Last, and so down to Longnose and round the North Foreland. This was familiar scenery, and for half an hour or so as we rounded the Foreland the visibility was at least two miles. But by the time we were off Ramsgate the fog had closed down again, and it persisted all the way into Dover.

Off the east entrance we obediently awaited the signal permitting us to enter, namely, two vertical red balls displayed on the control bridge, and then went in. If port control run up three balls in a triangle the message is 'no vessel may enter', and you just have to wait. Nowadays with the increasing and almost universal use of radio it is customary to call up port control and verbally request permission to enter, and any yacht relying on visual signals is regarded as being a little old fashioned. Nevertheless in we went, and proceeded as we had always done in the past into the Camber. This however did not please the authorities who shouted to us that we could on no account stay there and directed us to go to the other side of this huge harbour where we could anchor off the Prince of Wales Pier.

This we did and came to an anchor exactly at 15.00 hours, but there was a nasty swell in this part of the outer harbour, and we rolled and rolled in a most uncomfortable way. The alternative before us was to lock into the Wellington Dock, but the gates are only opened an hour to an hour and a half before high water, and HW Dover on this day was at 20.30, so that we were faced with several hours of discomfort. In the event we managed to get into the dock at 19.45 and tied up alongside the wall in a rather dirty and noisy corner, but where the water was at least calm. Our day's run had amounted to 58 miles, and again our average speed worked out at 8.3 knots.

The weather next morning was very similar, there was no wind and it was very misty, but it had the appearance of being a heat haze that might be expected to clear. The forecast was variable 2-3 becoming west force 4, and the sea was a flat oily calm. We left Dover soon after 09.00, and then I was guilty of two elementary but serious mistakes, for which we paid later on in the day. The first one was that I dithered about instead of taking full advantage of the west-going tide, with the result that instead of being at Dungeness by noon it was after 13.00 before we weathered it. The second was that I omitted to secure the anchor by lashing it to the rail which was the normal procedure, but left it lying on the foredeck. This was sheer carelessness, brought about by the fact that the sea had been flat calm for two days, and there seemed to be no indication of a change, but this is the sort of presumption that the sea does not permit or forgive.

From Dungeness to the Royal Sovereign light was about 24 miles and we covered this in three hours 25 minutes, but on the way there was a pretty steady deterioration in the weather. The visibility had improved but the wind had got up and by the time we reached the Royal Sovereign it was blowing about force 5-6 from the south west. The sea was also getting up and it was decidely choppy, but what was more serious was that the tide had turned against us and we were now struggling against a head sea as well as a strong head wind.

The next four hours are ones I would prefer to forget, for due to my poor seamanship we suffered. From the Royal Sovereign to Beachy Head the distance is only about seven miles, but it took us exactly three hours to weather the headland, and during that time we took a pounding. The sea was very rough and there was a large swell rolling in from the south-west. The sun was shining but was partially obscured by a fine haze and we were struggling directly into its path. The surface of the sea was white with streaked foam and had a ghostly silvery grey brilliance which dazzled the eye.

The noise of the wind and sea was deafening and almost drowned the sound of the engines, which fortunately never faltered, though we had to reduce the speed to 1500 rpm to prevent too much water coming aboard when she put her nose down into the waves. As it was, some salt water did find its way below, both fore and aft, and even into the wheelhouse via a ventilator which was immediately over the helmsman's seat.

Our offing from the headland was only about two miles, which was far too close — another elementary mistake — and at the height of the commotion the anchor suddenly slid across the deck towards the wheelhouse, dragging a length of chain behind it. There was nothing for it but to go out on deck and secure it before it did any damage or went over the side, and I had to leave Pat with the wheel and the struggle to keep her on course, which she did valiantly.

Narija also behaved well, though she did not like the ordeal to which we were subjecting her, but she coped with the conditions and was knocked down only once. Stowage, both above and below decks, was poor, and we were lucky not to have sustained more damage. In the event we lost the odd saucer, two mugs and a glass, and an Aladdin oil lamp, also a portable radio which bounced off its shelf.

After rounding Beachy we had another ten miles to go to Newhaven, and though it was still rough the sea conditions were not so violent and we made better progress. The log records these few hours as follows:

16.30 Royal Sovereign abeam. Sea Rough. Wind 5, possibly 6.
19.30 After 3 long hours, with worsening sea conditions, finally weathered Beachy with an offing of 2 miles. Too close?
21.10 Entered Newhaven, and glad of it.

Pat also has vivid recollections of this part of the trip, and remembers some of the frightening aspects of our experience that I had forgotten. She says:

> I remember the glassy calm surface of the sea turning into greasy heaving waves as we headed into the sun. As well as the plough anchor that was loose and slithering about the deck, and which I was sure was going to come crashing through into the wheelhouse, we were also worried about the dinghy which was in its chocks on the after coach roof, but which was not lashed down. As we were rolling quite considerably as well as pitching it seemed likely that the dinghy could shift and add to our troubles.
>
> I did not want Ron to go on deck in these conditions, believing he could well be washed overboard, but could see

> that the dinghy had to be lashed down, and that the anchor's suicidal gyrations on the foredeck had to be stopped. But I was very relieved when he had completed the task and was back inside the wheelhouse. With these two worries dealt with we were able to relax a little, and although the seas were mountainous we knew *Narija* would make it.

The next morning, after we had got our breath back, I added the following postscript to the log entry quoted above:

> One interesting reflection on the trip so far. Practically all the way from St Katherine's to Newhaven we have been steering into the sun, and even when we went into the Wellington Dock in Dover the sun was straight in our eyes. On the last lap, when we were having trouble in weathering Beachy Head, most of the time I was trying to steer straight into the path of the sun, which was very watery but had a beautiful moonlight effect on the grey water. Running through my head at this time was the hymn *Lead Kindly Light*. As we shaped up for Newhaven pierheads the sun was a huge red ball setting directly over the town, and it dropped out of sight at the moment we entered the haven.

We both had a strange feeling of being looked after, and this was heightened by the recollection that while we were struggling off Beachy Head we were conscious of a large naval type vessel a mile or two to the south'ard which was proceeding in the same direction. Although she disappeared from view when we were down in the troughs of the waves she seemed to be closing us and keeping station. She followed until we were within a mile or two of Newhaven, and it was very comforting to feel that perhaps we were being escorted. Just before we entered the harbour a Dieppe cross-Channel ferry came charging up behind us, but slowed down to let us get in first — so we were in fact escorted right into the harbour!

After this experience the rest of the voyage could be nothing but anti-climax. The final leg of sixty miles was calm and peaceful and we were soon back on our mooring in the River Yar. Though we had many other cruises in *Narija* we never subjected her, or ourselves, to those sort of conditions again, and I have never since gone to sea with my anchor lying loose on the foredeck.

The lesson to be learned from this little story is that you must always, but always, treat the sea with the greatest possible respect. The sea is there for us to appreciate and enjoy but it will not tolerate familiarities from mere puny mortals, and can so easily and quickly change from being a wonderful friend to a deadly and implacable enemy. If more yachtsmen understood this the lifeboat service would be far less busy.

Postscript

ON RETIREMENT, and after much cogitation, Pat and I decided to live in the Isle of Wight where the sailing is good, and where we already had friends. For a time we contemplated taking *Narija* down through the French canals for a long holiday in the Mediterranean, but for many reasons, which at the time seemed adequate, we changed our minds and settled down to a peaceful old age within sight and sound of the water.

Hindsight confirmed our decision to take things a little easier, and we continued to enjoy the various types of sailing available in the Solent area. Besides some gentle coastwise cruising we bought a sailing dinghy, called *Sae-Weod* (but inevitably always referred to as *Seaweed*), a 14-ft fibreglass boat that was a delight to sail and in which we enjoyed pottering about.

Anthony and Sally both married and soon had growing families, and every summer they all came down to the Island and we had a glorious fortnight camping and sailing in Newtown Harbour where the National Trust have a small and very secluded camping site. The children slept in tents, the grown ups in an old caravan belonging to the local farmer, and

Pat and I stayed on our boat anchored in the creek.

All my seven grandchildren learned to sail in the many fascinating creeks of Newtown, most of them in '*Seaweed*', and ultimately Anthony and his wife took over the boat while Sally and her husband bought a dinghy of their own. Anthony's eldest boy, Paul, became interested in traditional wooden boats as he grew older. He sailed a small gaff-rigged dinghy of his own and raced her very successfully against other similar boats in the Small Gaffers races held annually in the River Swale.

He also put pressure on his father to buy the fishing smack *Unity* which had fallen on hard times and was in poor condition, and between them they re-built and re-rigged her to a very high standard. Anthony by this time was very experienced in this type of work, for besides having converted the sailing barge *Lord Roberts* back to sail he had also restored the large smack *Rosa and Ada* which he bought in Whitstable where she had been lying derelict for two years.

Looking back over the sailing years — fifty of them — it is difficult to believe that all this nautical activity in my family of sailors should have started so casually one August day in 1939 when I was invited to try my hand at sailing a boat on the Norfolk Broads. It is impossible to describe the pleasure and satisfaction it gives me to know that the love of sailing created on that day is shared by the next two generations of my family. If those who read this book can also share this love, and can catch even a hint of the magic — just one whiff of the sea — from its pages, then this is a bonus. For me, Laurence Binyon summed it up with these words:

> What hour shall Fate in all the future find,
> Or what delights, even to equal these,
> Only to taste the warmth, the light, the wind,
> Only to be alive, and feel that life is sweet.

And sweet it can be for you too. You don't need lots of money; all you need is an old boat, a wooden boat, one that won't grumble at you if you put her aground, one in which you can wear your old clothes and feel the sun on your back, and hear the water lapping round the hull, one in which you can get away from the telephone, and the traffic, and be happy.

Index